TopGear
STIGtionary

BBC Children's Books
Published by the Penguin Group
Penguin Books Ltd, 80 Strand, London, WC2R 0RL, England
Penguin Group (Australia) Ltd, 250 Camberwell Road, Camberwell,
Victoria 3124, Australia (a division of Pearson Australia Group Pty Ltd)
Canada, India, New Zealand, South Africa

Published by BBC Children's Books, 2012
Text and design © Children's Character Books, 2012

001 – 10 9 8 7 6 5 4 3 2 1

Written by Sam Philip

ISBN: 978-1-40590-842-9

Printed in China

Shutterstock.com: Alexander Snahovskyy 98t, Alexander Tolstykh
146tl, Art Konovalov 143 tr, Brendan Howard 57mr, chatchai 39tl,
CHEN WS 99bl, Chris Green 72bl, cinemafestival 85b, cjmac 60bl,
Dariusz Majgier 170b, David Acosta Allely 17br & 101tr, DeepGreen
19b, Dikiiy 152t, Dongliu 44b & 174tr, DSPA 91tl, dutourdumonde
173mr (Stratos), Evren Kalinbacak 173tr, Featureflash 79t & 154bl,
fstockfoto 171tr, J. Henning Buchholz 149br, Jaggat 137tl & 140tl,
jbor 16bl, Joe Seer 141mr, Kanwarjit Singh Boparai 36tl, Max Earey
90br Max Earey 120b, MiAdS 173br, Migel 117bl, Mikael Hora 173mr
(snow), MountainHardcore 34mr, Naiyyer 120m, Nataliya Hora 168tl,
noomHH 36tr, PHB.cz (Richard Semik) 102t, Philip Lange 93b & 103t,
Rachael Russell 141b, Rihardz 157tr, skphotography 166b, Steve Mann
157b, Terry Straehley 41m, thelefty 163bl, Tupungato 123t, Tyler
Olsen 142t, Walter G Arce 57br & 108b, Yury Zakharov 92tr.

TopGear
STIGtionary

A definition of almost everything Top Gear

Introduction

In 1755, Dr Samuel Johnson compiled the first complete English dictionary. It took him over nine years to finish and defined nearly 43,000 words, and is regarded as the most important reference work in English history and one of the most ambitious books ever written.

Unfortunately, there was one big problem with Dr Johnson's dictionary: it didn't include cars, or *Top Gear*, anywhere at all. No mention of the Stig, no mention of the Bugatti Veyron, not even a mention of the Hammerhead Eagle iThrust.

OK, this might have had *something* to do with the fact that the Bugatti Veyron and Hammerhead Eagle iThrust wouldn't be invented for another 250 years (as for the Stig, we have no idea how old he is, or whether he was born, invented or mysteriously assembled himself from thin air). But that's surely Dr Johnson's fault for rushing his dictionary out the door before waiting to see if anything important was about to be invented, right?

So here's the solution to Dr Johnson's oversight, and to all those other dictionaries and encyclopedias that concern themselves with boring things like verbs and nouns and the textiles trade in the 14th century but completely ignore exciting things like Pagani Zondas and dropping a Volkswagon Beetle from a helicopter. It's called the Stigtionary, and it's your complete and exhaustive guide to everything *Top Gear*. Handily arranged in alphabetical format, it runs right the way from Abarth to Zetros, including the Caravan Airship, ducks, the Morris Marina and even torque along the way. If you've ever wondered what oversteer is, who the Bugatti test driver who stole James's speed record was, or how to spell that amazing Romanian mountain road declared by Jeremy as the greatest in the world, the Stigtionary holds the answer. Probably. Unless we forgot to put something in. Which we almost definitely didn't.

Aa

Abarth

An Italian race car maker established in 1948, Abarth was once famed for making fizzy little versions of the original 1960s Fiat 500, some with as much as… 27bhp! Nowadays, Abarth is best-known for building the…

Abarth 500C

It's based on the Fiat 500, but with loads

more power, big wheels and a funny sardine tin fabric roof. As Richard discovered in Italy, a surprising number of people will squeeze into an Abarth 500C.

ABS

Abbreviation for Anti-Lock Braking System. Fitted to almost all modern cars, ABS stops you from skidding when you hit the brakes by preventing the wheels from 'locking up' and sliding. However, it can't beat physics. If you've left it wayyyyy too late to brake for Gambon, ABS won't stop you from ending up in the grass.

> Fourteen! Count them up. That is magnificent!

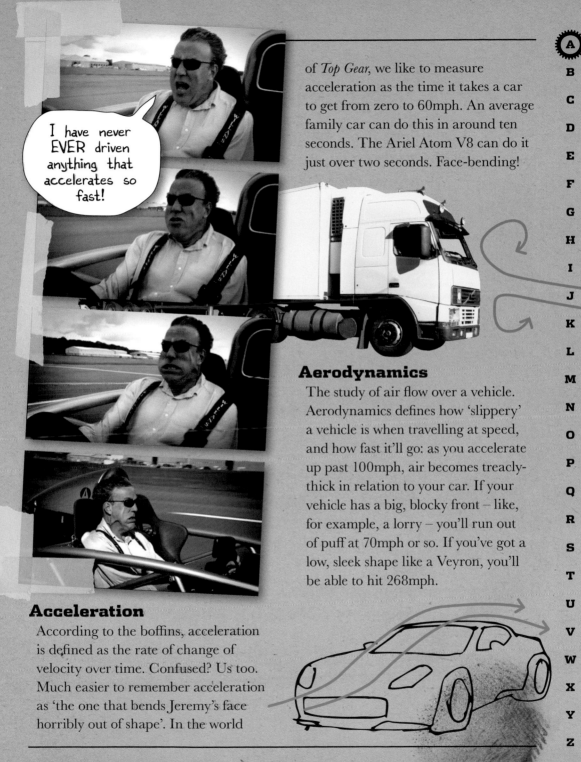

> I have never EVER driven anything that accelerates so fast!

of *Top Gear*, we like to measure acceleration as the time it takes a car to get from zero to 60mph. An average family car can do this in around ten seconds. The Ariel Atom V8 can do it just over two seconds. Face-bending!

Aerodynamics

The study of air flow over a vehicle. Aerodynamics defines how 'slippery' a vehicle is when travelling at speed, and how fast it'll go: as you accelerate up past 100mph, air becomes treacly-thick in relation to your car. If your vehicle has a big, blocky front – like, for example, a lorry – you'll run out of puff at 70mph or so. If you've got a low, sleek shape like a Veyron, you'll be able to hit 268mph.

Acceleration

According to the boffins, acceleration is defined as the rate of change of velocity over time. Confused? Us too. Much easier to remember acceleration as 'the one that bends Jeremy's face horribly out of shape'. In the world

Airbag

A safety device designed to stop the steering wheel hitting you in the face in the event of a crash. If your car detects you're having a collision, it will inflate rapidly to cushion the blow. They might look like big cuddly pillows, but be warned: airbags fire as quickly as a bullet from a gun.

Airport Vehicle Racing

Jumbo jets are fast, but if you've ever taken a plane journey, you'll know how painfully slow the gap between (a) arriving at the airport and (b) actually taking off can be. The problem? All those trundling airport vehicles: the ones that transport the fuel, the ones that move the bags around, the coaches to shuttle passengers from terminal to the plane. Richard decided there was only one way to speed this snailish process up: a race. More specifically, a race to find which airport vehicle was the fastest around a track. Don't say *Top Gear* never does anything useful…

Oh crikey, it's the Albanian rozzers!

Albania

A small country in south-eastern Europe, home to three million people and over four million goats. Albania is best known as one of Europe's poorest countries, the birthplace of Mother Teresa… and as an excellent place to test the performance of a trio of large luxury cars. But it's a very bad place to rob a bank: as James May found out, the Albanian police are VERY persistent.

Alfa Romeo

Italian maker of cars packed with beauty, soul and a wide array of electrical problems.

According to Jeremy, James and Richard, you can't be a true petrolhead unless you've owned an Alfa Romeo. The only problem with owning an Alfa Romeo is that it will probably break down. A lot. And leak a bit too. But at least it'll look pretty — especially if it's the…

Alfa Romeo 8C Competizione

"It's the best-looking car ever made!" sighed Clarkson when he tested the achingly gorgeous Alfa 8C back in 2009. The V8-engined, 450bhp 8C looks a million dollars, sounds a million dollars… but unfortunately drives like a pretty average Italian car. Do you really care?

altitude sickness can make you feel really not very well at all.

Amphibious car

Vehicle capable of travelling on both water and dry land. Throughout history there have been many attempts to build amphibious vehicles. Most of them have been quite rubbish and sinky. A few, like the Gibbs Aquada (below) in which multi-billionaire Richard Branson crossed the English Channel in just one hour and forty minutes back in 2004, have been not-too-bad. *Top Gear*'s several attempts at creating amphibious vehicles rank somewhere mid-table. Apart from Richard's 'DamperVan'. That was just rubbish.

Altitude sickness

Illness caused by lack of oxygen in the air in high mountains. As the boys discovered in the Andes,

Even if the cars could get over, which I seriously doubt, I can't. I'm calling it a day.

Amy Williams: Gold medal winner at tea-tray-skidding

Amy Williams

British sportswoman who won an Olympic gold medal in the skeleton in 2010. The skeleton is a stupid sport that involves sliding down an icy mountain on a tea tray. Amy might be quick, but she's not as fast as a Mini rally car.

And on that bombshell...

Jeremy's traditional ending to a *Top Gear* episode. The most important thing about Jeremy's 'bombshells' is that they must never, ever actually be useful, interesting or informative.

VS

Anne Hathaway's Cottage

The problem with car interiors, according to Jeremy, is that they're never as nice as your own house. So *Top Gear*'s trained buffoon decided to 'modify' a Mercedes S-Class to make it a bit more... homely. The result? A cabin with stone floors, a wood burner and a library. It was certainly cosy, but it wasn't fast. The car that Jeremy called 'Anne Hathaway's Cottage' – after the home of William Shakespeare's wife – took thirty-five seconds to reach 60mph.

If this goes any slower, we'll have to redecorate. It'll have gone out of fashion.

We're not just testing cars on this show, we're designing them. And on that bombshell, goodnight!

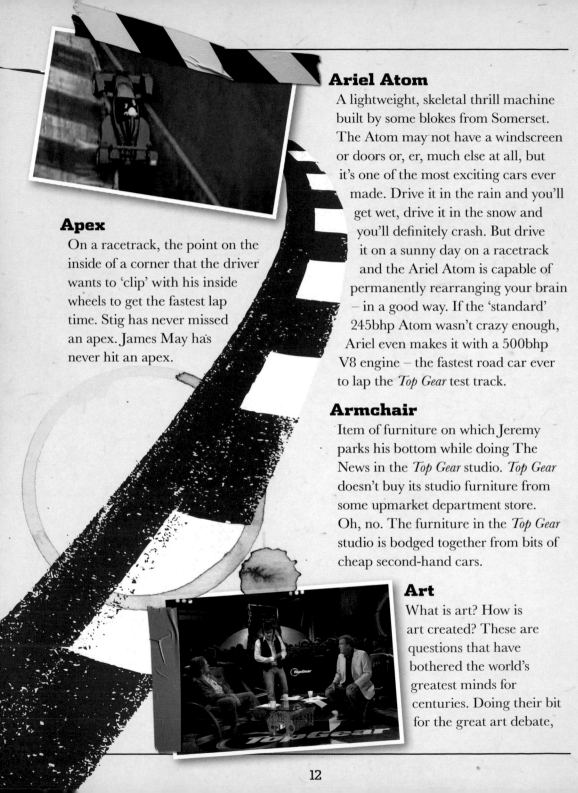

Ariel Atom

A lightweight, skeletal thrill machine built by some blokes from Somerset. The Atom may not have a windscreen or doors or, er, much else at all, but it's one of the most exciting cars ever made. Drive it in the rain and you'll get wet, drive it in the snow and you'll definitely crash. But drive it on a sunny day on a racetrack and the Ariel Atom is capable of permanently rearranging your brain – in a good way. If the 'standard' 245bhp Atom wasn't crazy enough, Ariel even makes it with a 500bhp V8 engine – the fastest road car ever to lap the *Top Gear* test track.

Apex

On a racetrack, the point on the inside of a corner that the driver wants to 'clip' with his inside wheels to get the fastest lap time. Stig has never missed an apex. James May has never hit an apex.

Armchair

Item of furniture on which Jeremy parks his bottom while doing The News in the *Top Gear* studio. *Top Gear* doesn't buy its studio furniture from some upmarket department store. Oh, no. The furniture in the *Top Gear* studio is bodged together from bits of cheap second-hand cars.

Art

What is art? How is art created? These are questions that have bothered the world's greatest minds for centuries. Doing their bit for the great art debate,

the boys took over a Middlesbrough gallery, filling it with car-related 'artworks', including a canvas splattered with paintballs fired from the exhaust of a Red Bull F1 car. As Jeremy will confirm, the greatest artists have to suffer for their work – he took a high-speed paintball to his gentleman's region!

Ascari

Tiny British supercar company that somehow manages to build some of the fastest, wildest vehicles on the planet. Ascari – named after Alberto Ascari, the Italian racer who became the first man to win the

F1 world championship twice – might be based in a small shed in Banbury, but it produces monsters like the A10 (above) which, thanks to its 625bhp V8 engine and a whole load of technology nicked straight from race cars, remains one of the fastest cars ever to tackle the TG track.

Aston Martin

Maker of jolly fine British sports
cars, founded in 1913 somewhere
in the Midlands. Since the 1950s,
Aston Martin has been renowned for
building some of the most beautiful
cars in the world – the DB4 of 1958
was a favourite of James
Bond, and even today
makes grown men go
all trembly in the knees.
007 is just as keen on the newest
crop of Aston Martins: it was a DBS
that was cruelly forced into a multiple
barrel roll in *Casino Royale*. Why do the
beautiful die so young?

Aston Martin DB9

Beautiful, sleek British sports car
with a mighty 6.0-litre V12 engine.
In the hands of Jeremy Clarkson, it
can get from the UK to Monte Carlo
quicker than James May and Richard
Hammond on the Eurostar.

it calls 'Quattro'. This means that fast Audis tend to be (a) very, very grippy and (b) not as keen on tyre-smoking as their BMW and Mercedes cousins.

Audi A8

A huge and luxurious executive car capable of getting from Edinburgh to London on just one tank of fuel… even in the hands of Jeremy 'Heavy Right Foot' Clarkson.

> I am absolutely lost for words. That is one astonishing car!

Aston Martin V8 Vantage N24

The stripped-out, strictly-no-air-con race version of Aston's V8 Vantage, driven by James on the boys' hunt to find Europe's best driving road. James ended up (a) very sweaty and (b) quite naked. Oh dear.

Audi R8 V10 Spyder

Sleek, sophisticated supercar convertible that oozes quality and class. Unless you've got long hair, that is…

Audi

German manufacturer of posh cars mainly driven by people who wear suits and play golf. Audi is famous for being one of the first manufacturers to put four-wheel drive on its road cars, and still fits all its fastest performance cars with the technology

> I don't like it!

> The Audi, then: not a good hairstylist.

Audi RS6 Avant

Freakishly large, freakishly powerful estate, armed with a 572bhp twin-turbo V10 and capable of 0-60mph in 4.6 seconds. But still slower down a snowy mountain than a pair of skiists…

Austin Allegro

Rubbish British family car from the 1970s that was rumoured to be more aerodynamic travelling backwards than forwards. Despite this, the Allegro failed to break the record for jumping-over-the-most-cars-while-travelling-in-reverse. Poor *Top Gear* Stunt Man…

Australia

Large, hot country on the wrong side of the planet, where people walk upside down and cook all their food in a strange device called the 'barbeque'. Australian cars tend to fall into two categories. One: pick-up trucks. Two: big floppy saloons with enormous V8 engines wedged under the bonnet.

Oh God we're
gonna die!

an accident at Italy's Imola circuit in 1994. If you think you've seen the 'Senna' name in F1 recently, you're right – Ayrton's nephew Bruno is one of the most promising young drivers on the grid.

As Jeremy, James and Richard discovered when they took on the presenters of *Top Gear* Australia in a series of completely-fair-and-definitely-not-fixed challenges, the Aussies are nowhere as good at driving as the British.

Automatic transmission

Transmission is a posh car engineer's word for 'gearbox'. An automatic transmission, then, is one that can change gears on its own, without the human behind the wheel needing to press a clutch pedal or waggle a gearstick. The best automatic transmissions can change gear super-smoothly and in the blink of an eye. The worst ones, however, will leave a car's passengers bobbing their heads back and forth like one of those nodding-dog toys…

Ayrton Senna

Probably the greatest driver in the history of Formula One. Senna won three F1 driver's titles between 1988 and 1991 before tragically dying in

Bruno Senna, 2012

17

Bb

BAC Mono

An amazing, lightweight British sports car most notable for having just one seat. As such, the Mono is the perfect car for the driver with no friends, the driver who shuns human company. A driver with superhuman skills but without the gift of speech. Anyone spring to mind?

Batteries

Lumps of engineering cleverness that store electricity. If you have an all-electric car such as the Nissan Leaf, it's the size and type of batteries that determine how far you can drive before having to recharge. As Jeremy and James discovered in Lincoln, most electric cars could do with bigger batteries.

Beef and onion crisps

James May's favourite flavour of crisps. Scientists have estimated that Captain Slow consumes over two thousand packets of beef and onion crisps each year.

Belgium

Small country located between France, Germany and Holland, and location of *Top Gear*'s 'World War' battle against Sabine Schmidt's German telly team. *Top Gear* won, of course.

Bentley

British maker of huge, glamorous cars favoured by Premiership footballists and pop stars. As well as dominating racing in the 1920s, the wealthy Bentley owners of the era invented their own '*Top Gear*' style challenges, racing their huge supercharged cars from the South of France to London against the fastest trains of the day. Of course, the car always won, beating public transport by just a few minutes. Sound familiar?

Bentley Brooklands

"This is a huge slab of old England!" bellowed Jeremy as he drifted the 530bhp super-coupé around the *Top Gear* track. Ten seconds later, the mighty Brooklands had devoured one of its own tyres…

It's a Yugo.

Yes. But in a number of critical ways, it's EXACTLY the same as the new Bentley Mulsanne.

things to them to make them fit for consumption by cars. As the boys discovered when they used their own biodiesel in the BritCar 24 Hour race, this sort of fuel can occasionally melt important bits of engines.

Bentley Mulsanne

Giant, luxurious four-door driven by James on *Top Gear*'s road trip around Albania. For a car that costs £220,000, we can't help thinking the Mulsanne looks a bit… like a battered old Yugo.

Billie Piper

Former pop star famous for (a) once being married to superstar ginger petrolhead Chris Evans and (b) getting lost on her lap of the *Top Gear* test track.

Lovely, lovely Billie

Biofuel

Fuel made from plant matter. Where most petrol and diesel is refined from crude oil drilled from deep under the surface of the earth, biofuel is made by harvesting crops – usually rapeseed or soy beans – and, erm, doing complicated chemical

> Our race chief reckoned we'd blown the turbo, the clutch and the flywheel.

Black Stig

The predecessor to White Stig, Black Stig featured in only the first two series of 'new' *Top Gear*. He disappeared trying to reach 100mph in a Jaguar XJS on the deck of *HMS Invincible*, a huge aircraft carrier. Unfortunately he couldn't come to a stop in time, plunged into the sea and hasn't been seen since. Some say he's still out there somewhere…

Blackpool

Seaside town in Northern England. As Richard and Jeremy proved, it is possible to drive all the way from Basel in Switzerland to Blackpool on just one tank of diesel… but only if you're very, very careful. And slow. And bored.

Blindness

Loss of sight in one or both eyes. As Billy Baxter proved, being blind doesn't stop you from lapping the *Top Gear* test track faster than Richard Whiteley or Terry Wogan.

> You OK? Phew, I'm not!

Bloodhound

British-built rocket car that aims to be the first vehicle to break 1000mph. Bloodhound is designed by the same team that created Thrust SSC, the first vehicle ever to break the sound barrier and still the holder of the land speed record. The Bloodhound team hope to break 1000mph some time in 2013. Fingers crossed they do it.

Blue Ridge Parkway

Scenic route in Virginia, USA, that is NOT the greatest driving road in the world. Because it's got a 45mph speed limit along its whole length.

The Blue Ridge Parkway is 469 miles long. It can't all be 45mph. Can't be.

BMW

German maker of some very, very fine cars. Bavarian Motor Works was established in 1917 in Munich building aircraft engines, but quickly decided cars were a much better idea. Today, BMW specialises in two very different sorts of cars: ultra-smooth, ultra-efficient diesels that will do a million miles to the gallon… and noisy, slidey rear-wheel drive performance cars like the M3. BMW also owns Mini and Rolls-Royce, but if you're from Britain you should probably stay quiet about that…

BMW M3

Tyre-smoking supersaloon that, despite packing a 414bhp V8, is actually more economical than a Toyota Prius around the *Top Gear* test track.

> It absolutely steals your heart.

BMW Z4M

338bhp roadster that, according to Hammond, is exactly like a very hot chilli. Presumably this is because if you add the BMW Z4M to your homemade curry, your mouth will hurt a lot.

Bobsleigh

An aerodynamic, very uncomfortable sled driven by unhinged men wearing lycra. As James and Richard discovered, bobsleighs are quicker at getting down mountains than Mitsubishi Evo rally cars. Only just, though.

Bolivia

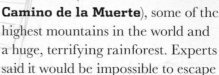

Small country in South America, home to ten million people, some of the most dangerous roads in the world (*see* **El Camino de la Muerte**), some of the highest mountains in the world and a huge, terrifying rainforest. Experts said it would be impossible to escape from the depths of the Bolivian jungle in a trio of second-hand cars bought for less than £3,500 each. As the boys proved, the experts were very nearly right. But somehow they survived the wildlife, the ravines and the rivers and made it to safety…

> Why did I listen to you, you imbecile?

> Our challenge was simple: see what speed we could achieve as we went past the mile marker . . . I'm not leaving here until I've achieved 170mph.

Bonneville Salt Flats

Huge, desolate salt pan in Utah, USA. Since the start of the twentieth century, Bonneville has been a leading location for land speed record attempts, thanks to its flat surface and lack of trees, cliffs and other things to crash into. In 1937, British daredevil Malcolm Campbell became the first man ever to reach 300mph in his Bluebird car on Bonneville Salt Flats. Just seventy-two years later, a bloke called Jeremy Clarkson broke the speed record for a production car at Bonneville in his Corvette ZR1…

Botswana

Country in Southern Africa full of sand and wild animals. Though similar in area to France, Botswana is home to just two million people, making it one of the emptiest countries on the planet. This means it is a very bad place to break down if you're, say, attempting to drive from one side of the country to the other in a battered old two-wheel drive car…

Bouncy castle

Large inflatable often seen at parties and fêtes. Thanks to vital scientific research by *Top Gear*, it is now known that bouncy castles are surprisingly difficult to jump over in ice cream vans.

Bowler Wildcat

"I am a driving god!" yelled Richard when he tested this indestructible off-roader back in 2003. Though the Wildcat is based on a Land Rover, it's no lazy mud-plugger: in fact, it'll do 0-60mph in under five seconds!

Britain

The greatest country in the universe, home to Stilton, Marmite, and, of course, *Top Gear*. Despite Britain not being the most enjoyable place in the world to drive – our roads are among the busiest on the planet, our fuel is expensive and speed cameras lurk around every corner – this plucky little island has still created some of the finest cars and drivers in history. Britain has produced ten winners of the Formula One drivers' championship: our nearest rival, Brazil, can boast just three. And which other nation makes cars as wonderful and exotic as Jaguars, Bentleys, Rolls-Royces and Caterhams? OK, OK, apart from Italy...

The E-type . . . is almost certainly the last truly great thing that Britain made. This is the soul, the spirit, the beating heart of all that we can be.

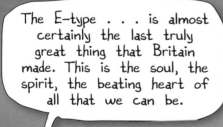

engine, while the 'Super Sport' packs 1,184bhp and will do 268mph flat-out. The Veyron will officially manage less than 10mpg (and a lot less than that if you're planning on finding out its top speed!), 0-62mph in 2.4 seconds and go from a standard start to 186mph in just 14.1 seconds. *Top Gear* loves the Veyron so much that it named the big Bugatti its car of last decade. Will there ever be another machine like it? Sadly, probably not…

British Racing Green

Britain's traditional racing colour. Britain's history of painting its race cars green stretches back over 100 years, to the very first international road races in history. France took blue, Germany got silver, and Britain – to pay respect Ireland, where the first race was held – went for green.

Bugatti Veyron

Quite simply the fastest road car in the world. The Veyron's vital statistics are staggering: the 'standard' version has a 1000bhp, 8.0-litre 16-cylinder

Build quality

Measure of how well a car has been constructed. Proper manufacturers test build quality by measuring the gaps between a car's panels, or checking how much noise it makes at speed using complicated, accurate instruments. *Top Gear* tests build quality by filling cars to the brim with water and then sending them off for a lap of the test track…

Mine doesn't fit.

Oh stop moaning!

Bullet Train

Known in Japan as the 'Shinkansen', the bullet train forms one of the fastest rail networks in the world. Capable of almost 200mph flat out, Japan's bullet trains carry over 150 million passengers between the country's cities every year. And they're never, ever late. But even the Shinkansen's amazing speed and regularity couldn't defeat Jeremy's Nissan GT-R in a race across Japan.

Bus racing

A lot of people think *Top Gear* hates public transport. Nothing could be further from the truth. *Top Gear* loves public transport. That's why, when he found out that London mayor Boris Johnson was searching for a new generation of buses for his city, Richard offered to discover which sort would be best for the job. By taking them all racing. There was a lot of crashing, all in the name of Important Research. Turns out the best bus for London is, erm… actually, we can't even remember which one won. Still, Important Research…

A common everyday scene from London's streets . . .

The best bus for London, or any other city, is the single decker, because it's quick.

29

Cc

Cadillac

Luxurious American manufacturer owned by General Motors. In the 1950s, Cadillac was famous for building huge, wafty pink convertibles with enormous tail fins. Nowadays Cadillac builds big V8 monsters like the CTS-V that James drove on the boys' Big American Muscle Car Road Trip.

Cabbie

Slang term for a taxi driver. To test the Renault Scenic and Ford C-Max back in 2004, James and Richard decided to pose as cabbies in South London. After a night of hen parties and fencing equipment, they decided they weren't really cut out for the world of minicabbing.

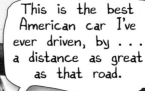

This is the best American car I've ever driven, by . . . a distance as great as that road.

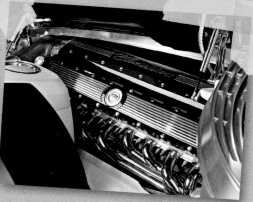

Cadillac Sixteen concept

A gargantuan supercar concept that, sadly, was never built. This is a pity: the Sixteen was fitted with a 13.6-litre V16 engine that produced 1000bhp!

Cadillac Type 53

Built in 1916, this was the first-ever car to boast the now-conventional three-pedal layout, with the clutch on the left, brake in the middle and accelerator on the right. This is the only interesting fact about the Cadillac Type 53.

Camping

An outdoor activity often involving tents, sleeping bags, camp fires and arguments. As James and Richard discovered when they took a bunch of convertibles on a big summer holiday in the Lake District, Britain really isn't a very good place for camping. Or convertibles. This is because, as you have probably noticed, Britain suffers from a lot of rain.

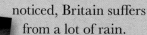

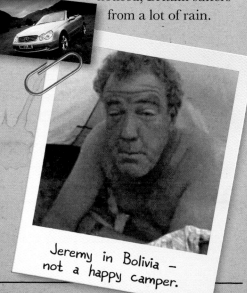

Jeremy in Bolivia – not a happy camper.

It's on fire. Run.

Caparo T1

"You can forget Enzos. You can forget Koenigseggs," yelled Jeremy as he thrashed the Caparo T1 on the *Top Gear* test track, "This is in a different league! This is acceleration like I have never ever experienced!"

It might look like an F1 car, but the amazing Caparo T1 is actually legal to drive on the road. With a 575bhp V8 engine behind the driver's head, and a 0-60mph time of under three seconds, you'll be quicker than anything else on the morning school run, but watch out for a couple of tiny issues. First, the T1 isn't very good at going round corners. And second, it does tend to break down rather a lot…

Car wash

A large and intricate contraption made of hoses and wires and brushes and soap. Automatic car washes are an excellent way of getting your grimy car sparkling-clean in just a couple of minutes. Unless your grimy car happens to be a home-made Renault Espace convertible…

Caravan

The sworn enemy of *Top Gear*. It is calculated that, in the last decade, *Top Gear* has destroyed over 300 caravans in fiery and inventive ways. Some people say *Top Gear* is unfairly cruel on caravans, but isn't it better that the big swaying menaces are providing entertainment to millions every Sunday evening rather than causing 20-mile tailbacks on every B-road in Britain throughout the summer?

Golf Papa Golf, I will attempt to clear your airspace. Please don't call the police.

Caravan Airship

What do you get if you cross a rickety caravan with a hot air balloon? The *Top Gear* caravan airship, that's what – one of the most innovative and successful uses for caravans ever devised. Not only does this clever invention keep caravans from clogging up our busy roads, it also provides passengers with beautiful views of the surrounding countryside. Watch out for crosswinds, though…

Caravanning

What people with caravans do. As Jeremy, James and Richard discovered when ordered by the *Top Gear* producers to go on a caravan holiday in Dorset, caravanning is slow, depressing, boring… and will almost inevitably end up with something catching on fire.

Caterham

Maker of lightweight sports cars that, through an amazing stroke of coincidence, is based in Caterham, Surrey. All Caterham's cars are based on the original Lotus Seven of 1957. Using a 50-year-old design, you might expect them to be slow and creaky, but you'd be wrong. Just look at the…

Caterham R500

One of the very fastest cars ever to go round the *Top Gear* track. Despite only producing 253bhp, the fact that the Caterham R500 weighs slightly less than a ballet shoe gives it blistering

All things considered, how do you think the holiday went?

acceleration and on-track performance to destroy cars costing five times as much…

Cessna 182

Four-seater light aeroplane, as flown by Captain James May in a race across France against the mighty Bugatti Veyron. Despite having a top speed of 173mph and the ability to fly at a height of nearly four miles above the earth, the Cessna was no match for the million-pound Veyron in the hands of Jeremy… though that might have had something to do with James's inability to fly at night!

You can't drive an offroad car fast over this kind of surface. You can in a tank!

Challenger tank

Big scary battle tank used by the British army. With a 26-litre, 1200bhp diesel engine, the Challenger is an awesome off-road vehicle: as Jeremy discovered, it's even more capable over rough ground than a Range Rover Sport! A bit trickier to park at Tesco, though…

Is that it? James, it's pathetic. It looks like something a builder would leave behind.

Chauffeur

The driver of a limousine. Chauffeurs should always be polite, well-dressed and never, ever get lost. When the boys used their home-made limousines to transport a trio of celebrities to the Brit Awards in 2007, they broke all three of these rules several times...

Chevrolet

In America, Chevrolet – one of General Motor's biggest brands – makes a bunch of cool muscle cars and trucks. In Europe, it puts its badge on a load of soggy city cars from South Korea, including the Lacetti, one of *TG*'s previous

Reasonably Priced Cars. *Top Gear* thinks this is unfair. *Top Gear* thinks Britain should get the Chevrolet Camaro and Corvette.

Chevrolet Camaro

American muscle car built since 1966, as driven by Jeremy on *Top Gear*'s Deep South road trip in 2007, and the fastest car in the hands of Big Stig...

Chevrolet Lacetti

Top Gear's former Reasonably Priced Car. Fifty-seven celebs took to the *Top Gear* track in the mighty Lacetti: the fastest of the bunch was Jay Kay with a blistering lap of 1:45.8...

I declare this lido open!

Chipping Norton lido

Outdoor swimming pool in the Oxfordshire village of Chipping Norton. In 2005, a local hooligan named Jeremy Clarkson drove a Rolls-Royce Silver Shadow into the lido. The locals were not impressed.

Chrysler

Along with Ford and GM, one of the US 'Big Three' car makers, and one of the largest manufacturers in the world. As well as building large, scary cars like the 300C, Chrysler also owns Dodge and Jeep and is closely related to Fiat. Oh, and until 2007 it was married to Mercedes. It's tough to keep up with all these relationships, isn't it?

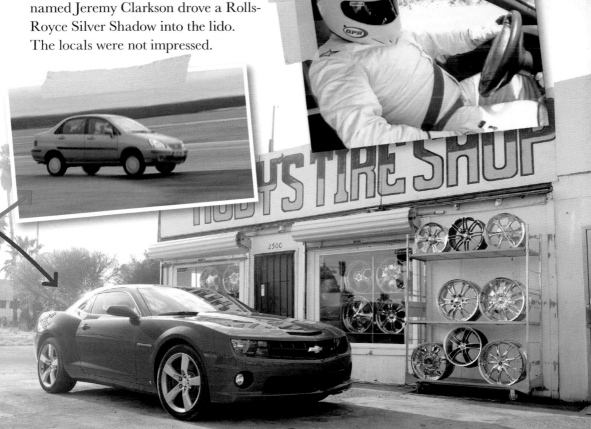

Citroën Ami

Rickety old French car, as driven by James May on the Mallorca classic rally. The Citroën Ami is not recognised as one of the great classic cars.

Chrysler Crossfire

An ugly coupé that Jeremy described as looking like "a dog doing a number two". It's safe to say he didn't like it much…

Citroën

French manufacturer of some of the weirdest cars in the universe. Citroën is most famous for building the 2CV in the 1950s, a back-to-basics machine that looked like an upside-down pram and could be driven across a ploughed field with a basket of eggs on the back seat without breaking any! Today, Citroën shares a lot of technology with its French neighbour Peugeot: for example, the Citroën C1 and Peugeot 107 are identical in everything but badge.

Citroën C1

Tiny city car that's less good at surviving Arctic temperatures than Richard Hammond.

Thirteen in a DS3 Racing. Beat that, Hammond!

Citroën DS3R

Fizzy orangey hot hatch driven by Jeremy on the boys' Monaco adventure in 2011. It may be a small car, but Jeremy somehow managed to squeeze thirteen people into his DS3R. Still that was one less than Hammond in his convertible Fiat 500!

Classic car

An old, collectible vehicle. The biggest problem with classic cars – apart from the fact that many of them are very keen on rusting and falling to pieces – is that no one can decide exactly what qualifies as a classic vehicle: some say it's a vehicle over twenty years old, some say it has to be over forty, some say it must have been built before 1973. All we know is that THIS is definitely a classic…

I've just done something . . . and I don't know what it was.

Classic rallying

Most rallying involves going as fast as possible. Not classic rallying. Classic rallying involves travelling between checkpoints in a precise time, matching the average speed set by the organisers. As Jeremy found on the boys' Mallorca rally adventure, this style of rallying does not suit his driving style.

Colin Chapman

Founder of Lotus and one of the greatest car engineers in history. Chapman's revolutionary F1 cars won dozens of Grands Prix in the 1960s, and his road cars were equally brilliant. He is most famous for coining the phrase "Simplify, and add lightness", which explains why even modern Lotus cars are light enough to blow away in a stiff breeze!

Concussion

A mild brain injury usually caused by a blow to the head. For example, a long-haired oaf might suffer concussion after being knocked over by a tow rope in the Syrian desert and banging his head on the ground…

Conkers

A traditional English game where players take turn to strike each other's conkers on a piece of string. Or, in the world of *Top Gear*, where players take turns to smash together caravans hung from cranes!

Convertible

Type of car with a roof that can be retracted and folded away. There are literally dozens of different sorts of convertible roofs – hard-tops, soft-tops, ones that fold automatically, ones that require the driver to dismantle them. Whatever flavour the convertible, it will always be girlier than its fixed-roof cousin!

Cool Wall, The

Top Gear's highly scientific method for determining how cool a vehicle is. Cars are ranked on the Cool Wall according to how much Jeremy thinks they would impress classy British actress Kristen Scott Thomas. The Cool Wall has four categories: Seriously Uncool, Uncool, Cool and Sub-Zero. For cars that are too cool for even the Sub-Zero category, on the right-hand side of the Cool Wall sits a fridge reserved for the very iciest cars in the universe. This fridge is full of Aston Martins. The most important rule of the Cool Wall is this: if one of Jeremy, James or Richard owns a car, it cannot be considered cool!

Cornwall

The most south-westerly county in Britain, and the boys' destination on their home-made motorhome challenge in 2010. Cornwall is well known for its tasty pasties, beautiful surfing beaches… and huge cliffs that will easily destroy a badly-parked three-storey Citroen.

Corvette

Brutish sports car produced by Chevrolet since 1953. The Corvette isn't sophisticated or subtle, but it's arguably the most important American sports car in history. When it was first built, the Corvette came with a 150bhp V8. Today, in 'ZR1' spec, it produces a snorting, supercharged 638bhp and can do 205mph flat-out, making it the fastest car General Motors has ever built. And General Motors has built a LOT of cars…

I'm starting to like this Corvette. It isn't the power, it's the surprise of the power.

With scenery like that, holidaying in England, even in a motorhome, does make sense.

Coupé

Traditionally, the word 'coupé' referred to a sporty two-door car: the Audi TT, for example, or Porsche Cayman. But recently manufacturers have been stretching the definition of the term: Mercedes calls its massive four-door CLS a coupé, and Audi reckons its big five-door A7 is a coupé too. Confused? Us too…

Cow

Large domesticated mammal often bred for meat or milk. As Jeremy discovered, if you are going to carry a cow on the roof of your Camaro, it is important to make sure it is securely strapped down.

Crash

A collision between two objects. In the world of *Top Gear*, these objects tend to be (a) two cars or (b) one car and something large and stationary. Over the years, the *Top Gear* presenters have become adept at crashing in a range of interesting and unusual ways.

Cylinder

The part of an engine where the magic happens: where fuel and air are combusted to create energy. As a general rule, the more cylinders an engine has, the more power it will produce: that's why a V12 engine (which has two banks of six cylinders arranged in a 'V' formation) is better than a boring four-cylinder engine from a family car…

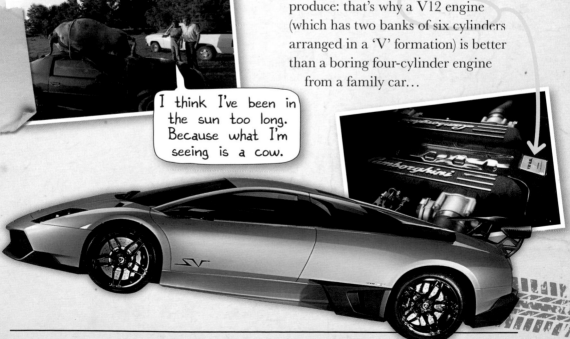

I think I've been in the sun too long. Because what I'm seeing is a cow.

Dd

Daihatsu Materia

Small Japanese minivan which, according to Jeremy, is slower, cheaper and easier to park than an Ascari A10. What would we do without him?

Daihatsu Terios

Small Japanese SUV that, despite Jeremy's best efforts to prove otherwise, can't outrun a traditional hunting outfit of horses and hounds.

Dampervan

Richard's amphibious vehicle, based on a VW Camper van. The Dampervan was wisely named: on its first outing on Rudyard reservoir, it sank immediately!

Dacia

Romanian budget brand owned by Renault. Dacia cars aren't beautiful or fast or even especially interesting, but for some reason James May seems to be obsessed by them, particularly the…

Dacia Sandero

Budget five-door hatchback that is completely unremarkable in every way, and may or may not be coming to the UK at some point. If you need more details on the Sandero, please ask Captain Slow.

Good news!

Deep South

The southern US states of Alabama, Georgia, Louisiana, Mississippi and South Carolina. People from the Deep South are often portrayed as hillbillies who play the banjo and chew straw. The boys found on their second-hand-car road trip through the Deep South, this couldn't be further from the truth. Erm, apart from one tiny incident at a gas station…

Diesel

Fuel traditionally used by trucks, tractors and ships. Once upon a time, diesel engines in cars were horribly slow, chugging lumps of pig-iron that sounded like rusty pneumatic drills. Nowadays, manufacturers like BMW are making diesels that are not only super-smooth and very nearly as quick as the most powerful petrol engines, but far more economical, too, meaning you can go miles further before having to visit the fuel station! And don't forget that every car that has won the Le Mans 24 Hour race since 2006 has been diesel-powered, too…

She said she was going to get the boys, so we decided to scarper!

A
B
C
D
E

I
J
K
L
M
N
O
P
Q
R
S
T
U
V
W
X
Y
Z

Dodge

American car maker owned by Chrysler. Most of the cars made by Dodge are big wagons for American soccer moms, or pick-up trucks driven by men called Bubba. But there's one exception to that rule: the insane Dodge Viper…

Dodge Challenger

The old-school orange muscle car driven by Richard on the boys'

American road trip in 2008. The Challenger is a very good car for doing huge, smoking burn-outs… unless you've got the automatic version!

Doggles

Goggles for canines, as worn by *Top Gear* Dog in 2006. For some reason these don't seem to have caught on at Crufts.

Can I crash into James's car every time we stop? Just a tiny bit?

Drifting

A tough-to-master technique where the driver intentionally oversteers to make the car go 'sideways'. There are a couple of important things to remember about drifting. First, it only works in a rear-wheel drive car: if your mum tries it in her Ford Focus she's going to look very silly. Second, you should never, ever try it on a public road, as you will crash and look even sillier.

Drive Time Radio

The 'prime time' radio slot, when most people are driving either to or from work. Drive time radio's most important job is to inform drivers of traffic jams or problems on the road, allowing them to avoid trouble and keeping the roads running smoothly. As the boys discovered when they hijacked Brighton's drive time radio in 2006, if you don't tell people about traffic jams, a very large area of the country can go into gridlock surprisingly quickly!

Drum kit

Jeremy's favourite musical instruments, presumably because they're (a) very noisy and (b) become quite annoying after a while. In 2008's lorry challenge, Jeremy was forced to make a hill start with his beloved drum kit parked directly behind his truck. Somehow he managed to pull away without reversing over his drums... but James and Richard destroyed them anyhow.

Ducks

Common aquatic bird of great interest to *Top Gear*'s tame racing driver. Some say he knows two facts about ducks, but both of them are wrong...

That wasn't meant to happen. I'll fade it out, and then you talk.

Ee

> That is a massive, massive drop!

Jeremy didn't enjoy the 600-metre vertical cliffs and gravelly single-lane track!

Edinburgh

Scotland's capital city. Edinburgh is exactly 400 miles from London, which means – as Jeremy discovered – you can drive all the way there and back on one tank of fuel… providing you're very careful on the throttle!

El Camino de la Muerte

Spanish for 'The Road of Death'. Running to La Paz in Bolivia, this forty-mile road is feared as the most dangerous in the world: as many as 300 travellers die driving it each year. When the boys tackled El Camino de la Muerte on their South American adventure,

Electric car

Vehicle driven by electric motors and powered by energy stored in batteries. Famous electric cars include the G-Wiz (which is rubbish) and the Tesla Roadster (which isn't). Many believe the electric car will save the planet as, for the most part, they're far cleaner and more eco-friendly than petrol or diesel cars. But they have a couple of tiny problems. Firstly, it depends where the

We now had a thirteen hour wait. Thankfully we were in Lincoln, where there are many things to see and do.

Emissions

Nasty stuff that comes out of a car's exhaust and contributes to air pollution. The most commonly measured emission from road cars is carbon dioxide, also known as CO_2 and measured in grams per kilometre (g/km). The more grams per kilometre of CO_2 a car produces, the more polluting it is: a Smart ForTwo diesel emits just 86g/km of CO_2, while a Lamborghini Aventador splutters out 398g/km of CO_2!

electricity has come from to run the car – if it's been generated by a solar panel or wind energy, brilliant, but if it's come from a coal power station, that's really not very clean at all. Secondly, as Jeremy and James discovered in Lincoln, it's very tough to fit an electric car with enough batteries to go for more than eighty miles or so before running out of juice. And, once you've run out of juice, it takes a VERY long time to recharge…

Ellen MacArthur

British sailor who, in 2005, broke the world record for sailing round the globe single-handed. A few months later, she set the fastest Star In A Reasonably Priced Car lap time around the *Top Gear* track in the Suzuki Liana. Not a bad year's work!

A
B
C
D
E
F
G
H
I
J
K
L
M
N
O
P
Q
R
S
T
U
Y
Z

Yeess! You BRILLIANT little car. God this is just brilliant. That's absolutely epic.

English Channel

Body of water separating England from France, conquered by Jeremy's amphibious 'Nissank' in 2007. And a few hundred swimmers over the years, which is more impressive, really.

Endurance racing

Form of racing where teams aim to either cover a large distance (usually 1000km or 1000 miles) as quickly as possible, or complete the most laps over a set period of time, usually either twelve or twenty-four hours. Endurance racing tests cars and drivers to the very limit – and often beyond! The most famous endurance race in the world is the 24 Hours of Le Mans, which is held every June in France and is usually won by a diesel Audi. The boys had their own shot at endurance racing in the slightly-less-glamorous BritCar 24 Hour in their BMW 3-Series running on biofuel. As Jeremy will confirm, endurance racing can be an emotional experience…

Eurofighter Typhoon

Fighter jet capable of 1,550mph and one of the very few things in the world capable of beating a Bugatti Veyron in a sprint. When Richard stupidly challenged the Typhoon to a two-mile drag race, he thought he might have a chance as the plane would have to climb a vertical mile in the air before turning round and returning to earth, while the Veyron would simply have to blast a mile up a runway, turn and blast back down. However, Richard hadn't reckoned on the blistering acceleration of the £67m Typhoon. The million-pound Veyron was simply blown away!

Exhaust

The system of piping that takes burnt gas away from an engine in a car. Exhausts perform a vital role in keeping the engine running efficiently and at the right temperature. But, far more importantly, if they're big enough and connected up to a shouty supercar engine, they can sound AMAZING!

Eyjafjallajökull

The unpronounceable Icelandic volcano visited by James May in a Toyota Hilux in 2010. Just a few weeks after Captain Slow's visit, Eyjawotsit erupted in spectacular fashion, covering Iceland in volcanic ash and grounding most of Europe's planes. James claims he wasn't responsible for the eruption, but that can't be a simple coincidence, can it?

Traction control off. Gearbox to manual. Launch control . . . left foot on brake, give it the full beans on the throttle. This is it!

Ff

Opened in 1937, the Golden Gate Bridge is much like the Humber Bridge in Britain, only smaller.

Factual

What *Top Gear* is. At least, what *Top Gear* has to be when it visits the United States. When Jeremy, James and Richard went on their muscle car road trip to Bonneville Salt Flats, the US government would only give them visas to film a factual programme, not an entertainment programme. This meant they weren't allowed to be silly. Obviously this was no problem at all…

Ferrari

Italian manufacturer of the greatest supercars in the world. Scuderia Ferrari (Scuderia is Italian for 'team') was founded in Maranello in 1929, but didn't leap to international fame until the birth of Formula One in 1950. Ferrari won its first F1 race in 1951 and hasn't looked back since: it has more race wins than any other manufacturer and is the only team to compete in EVERY F1 season since 1950! Between 1949 and 1965 Ferrari also won the prestigious 24 Hours of Le Mans endurance race nine times – only Porsche and Audi have recorded more victories. Ferrari's road cars are among the most exotic and expensive on the planet: in August 2011, a beautiful 1957 Testa Rossa sold for $16.4m, the highest price ever paid for a car at auction.

Ferrari 458 Italia

Maranello's latest mid-engined supercar is one of the finest Ferraris in history. Its 4.5-litre V8 engine makes 562bhp, it'll do 0-62mph in 3.4 seconds and 202mph flat-out. More importantly, it's so pretty that Jeremy described its front end as looking like 'Kristen Scott-Thomas's cheekbones'.

Ferrari 599 GTO

The most powerful road car Ferrari has ever built. The GTO is the faster, harder version of the lovely 599, with handling so scary that Jeremy described it as "not a car, but a wild animal!"

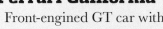

Ferrari California

Front-engined GT car with a folding hard-top roof, as driven by Richard on the boys' Romanian road trip. Some people say the California is too soft to be a Ferrari, but once you've heard that big V8 engine howling through a tunnel, you won't care!

This is a whole new type of car for Ferrari.

but despite its 175mph top speed couldn't beat James in a million-pound powerboat.

Ferrari F40

The greatest supercar of all time. First built in 1987, the 470bhp twin-turbo F40 was the first road car ever to crack 200mph, and remains one of the most hardcore, scary machines ever built. Just 1,300 F40s were made, and though they cost an, erm, mere £300,000 new, a clean example today will set you back over a million pounds!

Ferrari FXX

Based on the amazing street-legal Enzo, the FXX is one of the most extreme hypercars in history. Michael

> If James wanted a race, he'd get one. 4.4-litre Italian V12 unleashed. Ha haaa!

Ferrari Daytona

Classic Ferrari GT car built between 1968 and 1973. To celebrate the Daytona's fortieth birthday, Richard drove one along the French Riviera,

Fiat

Italian manufacturer that for many years made interesting, cheap city cars that fell to pieces at the first sign of rain. Nowadays, Fiat makes interesting, cheap city cars that don't fall to pieces at the first sign of rain. Fiat's greatest-ever hit was the 500 of 1957, a tiny, budget runabout that sold millions around the globe. In 2007, Fiat reinvented its original hit with the…

Schumacher drove his personal FXX round the *Top Gear* test track in just 1m10.7s – but the lap time didn't make the official board as the car isn't road-legal.

Fiat 500

Cute little car favoured by estate agents, fashionable London types and Richard Hammond. Much more manly in Abarth flavour…

Old Fiat 500 – small and fun

New Fiat 500 – small and LOTS of fun

Fiat Panda

A blocky, budget Italian city car
much loved by James May. In fact,
while Jeremy and Richard were
buying Lamborghinis and Mustangs,
Captain Slow treated himself to a nice
sensible Panda. Not to be confused
with the bamboo-eating Chinese bear,
which is slower and furrier.

Finland

Country in northern Scandinavia
that, for reasons that have confounded
scientists for decades, produces the
greatest racing drivers in the world.
Since 1977, Finnish drivers have
won the World Rally Championship
fourteen times, compared to just two
titles for British drivers. Not bad for a
country of just five million people!

You did it! That's the Finnish way.

Tervetuloa Suomi!
(Welcome to Finland)

Follow Through

The fastest section of the *Top Gear* test track, so called because that's what you might do if you take it flat out!

Football

Sport traditionally played by two teams of eleven men, using a small round ball. But, in the world of *Top Gear*, a sport played by two teams of five dinky city cars, using a very large ball and involving an awful lot of crashing.

Yeesss!

Ford

One of the American 'Big Three' and 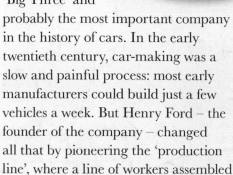 probably the most important company in the history of cars. In the early twentieth century, car-making was a slow and painful process: most early manufacturers could build just a few vehicles a week. But Henry Ford – the founder of the company – changed all that by pioneering the 'production line', where a line of workers assembled cars as they moved through the factory. Ford cut the time taken to make a car from thirteen hours to just an hour and a half, and by 1915 was making half a  million cars a year! In the late 1960s, Ford dominated the Le Mans 24 Hour race, winning four years on the trot. Today, it makes some of the best-driving cheap cars in the world…

Ford GT

Old-school modern supercar that echoes Ford's original 'GT40' supercar of the 1960s. Jeremy loved the new Ford GT so much that he bought one. Problem is, the 550bhp GT has a fuel tank the size of a pygmy hedgehog.

The petrol station – the natural home territory for the Ford GT. There it is, drinking its fill for the forty-seventh time today.

Ford Fiesta

Small, sensible city car that's excellent for evading Corvette-driving baddies in a shopping centre and assisting the Royal Marines with a beach landing.

The GT390 is, in car terms, one of the seven wonders of the world. The noise, the presence . . .

Ford Mustang

Classic American muscle car first built in 1964. *Top Gear*'s resident muscle car enthusiast Richard Hammond owns an original Mustang GT390 which, in its day, made 325bhp. Today? Just 250bhp. Poor Hammond.

Ford Sierra Estate

Family wagon used by *Top Gear* to set a new Guinness World Record for the most barrel rolls performed by a car. The plucky Sierra managed six complete rolls, but didn't look too good by the end of it…

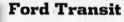

Ford Transit

Big van usually driven by builders. Also capable of lapping the Nürburgring in just ten minutes… in the hands of Sabine Schmitz, at least.

That was the hardest race of my life!

The power-to-weight ratio of this is 1,500 horsepower per ton!

It's just so . . . There's so much to learn! I can't drive fast enough.

Formula One

The most advanced, fastest and best single-seat racing series In The World. F1 cars are scarily powerful – as much as 800bhp – and scarily light, weighing less than a quarter as much as a Bugatti Veyron. This means they're scorchingly quick but very tough to drive. As Richard Hammond discovered when he attempted to wrestle Renault's championship-winning car around Silverstone, driving an F1 car is far, far more difficult than it looks!

France

Large European country handily located just to the south of England, best known for making cheese, wine and interesting cars that often fall apart. Though French manufacturers are renowned for building excellent hot hatches – from the

old Peugeot 205 GTi to the modern Renaultsport Clio 200, the car James drove around the Monaco Grand Prix circuit – for some reason no one in France actually cares about fast cars. Everyone in France drives a battered old diesel with several dents in every panel...

Fuel economy

Measure of how far a car will travel on a given quantity of fuel, usually a gallon. A car that can go sixty miles on a gallon of fuel is three times more economical than a car that can only do twenty miles. Fast, heavy cars tend to be less economical than small, light cars. In the UK, manufacturers are legally required to advertise the fuel economy of their cars, but you'd have to have feet as feathery as a ballerina to get anywhere near the quoted figure of most cars.

There's a price to pay for all that speed: catastrophic understeer.

Front-wheel drive

The most common 'drivetrain' layout, where the engine drives a car's front wheels only. Most small city cars use front-wheel drive, but it is very rarely found on supercars, which tend to be rear- or four-wheel drive. This is because powerful front-wheel drive cars usually suffer from torque steer and understeer.

Gg

Gambon

The last corner of the *Top Gear* test track, named after actor Michael Gambon who was the first to take it on two wheels in the Reasonably Priced Car.

G-Wiz

Horrible little electric car that doesn't have to pass crash tests because it's apparently a 'quadricycle' and not a car. This means you do not want to have a crash in a G-Wiz. Even with *Top Gear*'s finest modifications (mainly consisting of lots and lots of extra batteries), a remote-controlled G-Wiz is still slower than a £30 kids' toy.

General Motors

The biggest of the USA's 'Big Three' car makers. Commonly shorted to 'GM', General Motors is based in Detroit and owns dozens of brands including Cadillac, Chevrolet and Buick in the USA, Holden in Australia, Opel in Europe and Vauxhall in the UK. In 2011, GM sold nine million cars and trucks around the globe, beating Toyota and Volkswagen to become the biggest manufacturer in the world. Over the last century, GM has built literally hundreds of millions of cars, but do you know which was the most powerful? The 638bhp Corvette ZR1 driven by Jeremy on the Bonneville Salt Flats…

Well, you got the fastest run we ever clocked on these clocks.

I can't stop it! You [beep], what have you done?

stretches of motorway without speed limits. Yes, that's right – on certain public roads in Germany, you can drive as fast as you like. If you needed any more proof of Germany's obsession with going VERY FAST, don't forget it's also home to the terrifying 'Nürburgring' race track…

Genesis

Old British pop-rock band hated by Richard. That's why James and Jeremy keep 'modifying' the stereos on Richard's cars to only play Genesis at VERY LOUD VOLUME!

Germany

Large European country fond of sports cars, sausages and driving very fast. Germany is the birthplace of some of the best cars in the world – including Porsches, BMWs, Mercedes and Audis – but also the autobahns:

Greenhouse gases

Harmful exhaust gases so-called because they trap heat within Earth's atmosphere, warming the planet like a greenhouse. As Jeremy found out, attempting to solve the problem of greenhouses gases by fitting an ACTUAL greenhouse to the back of a Range Rover doesn't quite work.

Greyhound

Second-fastest accelerating creature on the planet, just behind the cheetah. A greyhound is faster round a dirt track than a Mazda MX-5 with Richard behind the wheel…

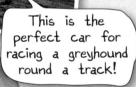

This is the perfect car for racing a greyhound round a track!

GTO

Abbreviation of Gran Turismo Omologati – that's Italian for 'Grand Touring Homologation'. The GTO badge is used by Ferrari on its most extreme road-going creations: in fact, only three cars have been badged GTO in Ferrari's eighty year history. The most recent of these was the homicidal 599 GTO (*see page 53*)…

Gullwing doors

Doors that hinge upwards from the centre of the car's roof, as seen on the Mercedes SLS. Gullwings are

Gumpert Apollo

Absurd, absurdly-named German hypercar capable of (a) doing 224mph and (b) scaring small children with its big ugly face. You can adjust almost every bit of the £250,000 twin-turbo Apollo – the suspension, the dampers, the traction control – but there are two things you can't alter. Firstly, that daft name, and secondly the looks: Richard described the Gumpert as 'a boil on the buttock of a baboon'!

called gullwings because they, er, look like a seagull's wings. You'd guessed that, right? Gullwings are not to be confused with scissor doors, as seen on the Lamborghini Murcielago…

It's got looks only a mother could love and a name like a Northern comedian.

Hh

be classed as a true hairpin. On the amazing **Stelvio Pass** (*see page 147*) there are forty-eight hairpins!

Hair omelette

As you might have guessed, an omelette made of hair. Jeremy had to eat a hair omelette in 2004 after betting that the production Vauxhall Astra wouldn't look like the concept. It did.

Hairpin

On a racetrack, a corner that bends right back on itself, like a metal hair clip. The closest thing to a hairpin on the *Top Gear* test track is the Hammerhead corner, which doesn't quite double back on itself enough to

Hammer

Heavy tool used by carpenters to bash nails into lumps of wood, and by Jeremy to fix literally anything that's broken. Sure, qualified mechanics might insist you need a range of

Now that's what I'm talking about! That's how to build a car. [BANG!] Ah. Broken.

spanners, screwdrivers and wrenches to fix a blown head gasket, but Jeremy maintains everything can be fixed by repeated whacking with a hammer.

Hammerhead

The tightest corner on the *Top Gear* test track, named for its not-very-close resemblance to the top end of a hammerhead shark.

James, the chimney's come off. There's quite a lot of smoke in here.

This does not look like the *Top Gear* track.

Hammerhead Eagle iThrust

Top Gear's home-made electric car, also known as Geoff. The Hammerhead Eagle iThrust used the chassis from a TVR, the electric motor from a milk float and a diesel generator to recharge its batteries. Though undoubtedly a unique and visionary creation, the iThrust did suffer a few tiny problems, especially with fumes from the diesel generator, which often choked the driver and passengers. It was these fumes that killed Green Stig…

Would you buy a kit car that I'd built?

Handbrake

Latching brake used to stop the car rolling off when stopped on a hill. As James discovered on the boys' big lorry challenge, some handbrakes are more difficult to use than others! (*see* **Hill start**)

Hat

Piece of clothing worn on the head for protection, warmth or fashion reasons. In the last decade of *Top Gear*, the *Top Gear* presenters have worn an array of

I'm wearing this hat so gypsies think I'm . . . a lucky, pools-winning gypsy.

truly ridiculous hats. Here are some of the silliest…

Hawk Stratos

The Lancia Stratos was one of the most brilliant Italian cars of the 1970s. Problem is, to buy one today would cost you at least £100,000. What could be better, then, than a perfect kit-car replica of the original Stratos for just £13,000? Lots of things, as it turns out. A bout of shingles, for one. Or falling down a flight of stairs…

Hill start

If you're parked facing uphill on a steep slope, it can be tricky to balance clutch, accelerator and handbrake to make a smooth getaway without rolling backwards – a perfect hill start. As James May will attest, it's even more difficult if you're attempting a hill start in a seven-tonne lorry with your beloved piano parked directly behind it!

Honda

Japanese manufacturer of clever, technological little cars and some excellent sporty stuff, too. Honda's greatest hits include the amazing NSX supercar of 1990 – which was developed by **Ayrton Senna** (*see page 17*) – and the manic, high-revving S2000 roadster which even today remains one of the very finest cars in which to teach grannies to do doughnuts…

Honda FCX Clarity

A futuristic fuel-cell car, and one of the first in the world to be powered by **hydrogen** (*see page 70*). And the saviour of the universe, according to James May.

Hummer

American maker of giant SUVs, which sadly died in 2010. Hummer started off converting huge US military trucks for American buyers who felt normal V8 pick-ups to be too small and quiet. One of the most famous Hummer owners is Arnold 'The Terminator' Schwarzenegger, who converted his car to run on hydrogen after discovering a three-tonne truck with a V8 engine wasn't really very environmentally friendly at all…

Honestly, I'd rather look at a baboon. In fact, come to think of it, I'd rather look at the back of a baboon.

Hybrid

A car that uses a combination of electric and petrol (or diesel) power, usually in the name of saving the planet. The most famous hybrid, of course, is the **Toyota Prius** (*see page 158*), which Jeremy described as 'one of my least favourite cars in the world'. Many are convinced that hybrids are the most environmentally friendly cars because they can run on electric power alone when pottering through traffic, meaning no nasty petrol or diesel emissions. However, others (Mr Clarkson included) argue that it's not very environmentally friendly to (a) build a battery pack in the first place and then (b) lug it around everywhere in your car, and that you'd be much better off with a nice, clean diesel instead.
Fight on!

Hydrogen

The most common element in the universe, and the fuel that might just save the world, if you believe James May. Cars like the Honda FCX Clarity run off electricity made by combining hydrogen (kept in compressed form in the fuel tank) and oxygen (from the air). While normal petrol and diesel cars produce all sorts of nasty emissions and greenhouse gases, the only waste product emitted by a hydrogen car is… water. And, unlike electric cars like the **Nissan Leaf** (*see page 109*), hydrogen cars don't take hours to recharge, as they don't have any batteries.

To refuel, all you need to do is refill your tank with hydrogen. The only problem is finding a fuel station with a hydrogen pump. In Britain, there are no fuel stations with hydrogen pumps. Ah.

Hypercars

The fastest, wildest, most expensive vehicles on the planet. If you're confused by the difference between supercars and hypercars, here's how to tell. Picture a car. Can you imagine driving it into the middle of London and parking it outside a posh restaurant to admiring glances from the other diners? Yes? Then it's a supercar. Is it far too expensive and impractical to park on the street without crashing into at least half a dozen cars and possibly setting on fire? Yes? Then it's

a hypercar. To put it another way, the Lamborghini Gallardo is a supercar. The Lamborghini Murcielago SV is a hypercar. *Top Gear* loves hypercars.

Hyundai

South Korean manufacturer that once made embarrassing, tinny cars, but now makes very-good-and-reliable-and-well-priced-but-slightly-boring cars. Hyundai is the sister firm of Kia: in fact, the Hyundai i30 is all but identical to the C'eed, *Top Gear*'s current Reasonably Priced Car. Good to know there's a Reasonably Priced Alternative…

From every angle, this looks absolutely evil.

Ii

> So there you have it – the future of motoring. Unless you're fat.

I-Real
Electric throne-with-wheels that Toyota claims is the future of motoring. Richard wasn't quite so convinced…

Ice hockey
Winter sport in which two teams of six men skate around and smash into each other while pretending to play hockey. Or, in *Top Gear* world, a winter sport in which two teams of Suzuki Swifts skate around and smash into each other while pretending to play hockey.

Ice racing
The slipperiest form of motorsport… in the world. Racing on a frozen lake requires Stig-like driving skills and a delicately-balanced car. As the boys discovered in Val Thorens, ice racing is very difficult in a trio of battered £1,500 rear-wheel drive coupés…

Ice cream van
Commercial vehicle that sells frozen confectionery and is not very good at jumping over **bouncy castles** (*see page 24*).

> And they're off! Well, he is, anyway.

Ice-skating

Winter Olympic sport in which skaters reach speeds of over 40mph on a cold, hard, bone-shattering surface. Ice-skating is a faster way of crossing a lake than driving a Jaguar XK…

Iceland

Chilly island in the north Atlantic most famous for (a) some rather lively volcanic activity (see **Eyjafjallajökull**) and (b) being an excellent country to test out convertible coupés like the Chrysler Crossfire, Nissan 350Z and Audi TT. Iceland is also a very good place to race a modified off-roader against a snowmobile… across a lake.

India

By population, the second-biggest country in the world, and home to the some of its most dangerous roads. Along with China, India is one of the world's up-and-coming superpowers, and Indians are buying more cars than almost anyone else: over two million in 2010 alone! Deciding that Britain should get in on India's newfound wealth, the boys decided to stage a 'trade mission' to the country, in which they drove around India in a few of Britain's finest cars: a Jaguar XJS, a Rolls-Royce Silver Shadow and a Mini Cooper. After failing to deliver packed lunches in Mumbai, accidentally winning their own hill climb event in Jaipur and nearly blowing up a posh garden party with fireworks in Delhi, they decided that diplomatic missions might be better left to the professionals…

> This is something I think could sell well in India.

A B C D E F G H I J K L M N O P Q R S T U V W X Y Z

Indoor World Speed Record

Just one of many world records held by *Top Gear*. In 2006, The Stig drove a Toyota F1 car to 81mph in London's ExCeL centre. Doesn't sound very fast, does it? Well, it isn't. But since no one had bothered to set an indoor speed record before, it put *Top Gear* in the record books...

Infiniti

Nissan's luxury brand, like Lexus for Toyota. Infiniti makes some very posh but very ugly cars, like the whale-faced FX 4x4...

Iran

Large country in the Middle East from which *Top Gear* is banned for 'political reasons'. In fact, the whole of the BBC is banned from Iran for political reasons and, as Jeremy discovered when the boys tried to cross the border from Iraq into Iran, this ban includes silly BBC2 shows about motor vehicles...

> Bad news. We can't cross the border.

Isle of Man

Small island in the Irish Sea between England and Northern Ireland. Though only thirty miles long and home to just

85,000 people, the Isle of Man is very significant in the world of petrolheads for one very important reason: some of its roads have no speed limits. This makes it an excellent place to test fast cars like the Aston Martin V8 Vantage, BMW M6 and Porsche 911. In fact, it's such a good place to test cars that Jeremy bought a house on the island. Each year, the Isle of Man also hosts one of the scariest motorcycle races on earth: the TT (Tourist Trophy) a thirty-eight mile lap around the island on public roads, at average speeds over 130mph...

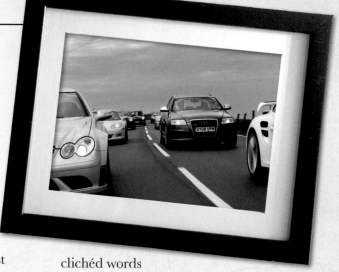

Italian Car Road Test Cliché Swear Box

Piggy bank into which *Top Gear* presenters must place a pound if they describe an Italian car using any clichéd words like 'soul' or 'passion'. That'll be two pounds right there.

Italy

Large European country that invented pasta, pizza and supercars. Italy is home to Alfa Romeo, Lancia, Lamborghini and Pagani, all companies allergic to building ugly, boring cars. Why do Italians build more exciting cars than, say, the French or the Germans? No one really knows, but we suspect it might have something to do with the nice weather. Or the food. Actually, we have no idea. Italy is also one of the most successful motorsport nations in the world, mainly thanks to a certain small company called Ferrari...

The danger is it will have lost its essential Alfa you-know-what, and it won't drive with all the traditional Alfa diddly and doodah.

Jj

I'd be surprised if you didn't turn out to be better than the other two.

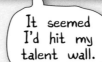

Jackie Stewart

Scottish racing driver who won three F1 drivers' championships between 1969 and 1973, and even turned Captain Slow into a proper racing driver with a day of hands-on tuition around a race track in a TVR Tuscan! James might be a little embarrassed that he referred to Sir Jackie as 'a Scottish lady'…

It seemed I'd hit my talent wall.

Jaguar

British manufacturer with a fine pedigree of making fast cars. Way back in 1948, Jaguar built the beautiful XK120, the first road car capable of doing 120mph. Yes, that's the car in which James May beat Jeremy in a steam train and Richard on a 1940s motorbike from London to Edinburgh! Forty-four years later, in 1992, Jaguar broke another speed record when it released the

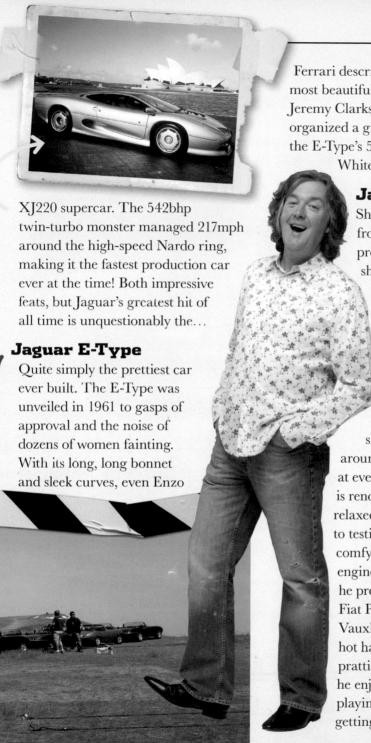

Ferrari described the E-Type as 'the most beautiful car ever made', and Jeremy Clarkson agreed. In 2011, JC organized a giant tribute in honour of the E-Type's 50th anniversary on the White Cliffs of Dover.

James May

Shaggy-haired bloke from London often seen presenting *Top Gear* or shows about machinery, toys and man-stuff. Despite being widely known as 'Captain Slow', James May is not a real captain. Where Jeremy and Richard are obsessed with power sliding supercars around the *Top Gear* track at every opportunity, James is renowned for his more relaxed, intellectual approach to testing cars. He loves a comfy ride and interesting engineering, which is why he prefers the two-cylinder Fiat Panda to the snorting Vauxhall Corsa Nürburgring hot hatch. When James isn't pratting around on *Top Gear*, he enjoys fixing motorcycles, playing the piano and getting lost.

XJ220 supercar. The 542bhp twin-turbo monster managed 217mph around the high-speed Nardo ring, making it the fastest production car ever at the time! Both impressive feats, but Jaguar's greatest hit of all time is unquestionably the…

Jaguar E-Type

Quite simply the prettiest car ever built. The E-Type was unveiled in 1961 to gasps of approval and the noise of dozens of women fainting. With its long, long bonnet and sleek curves, even Enzo

A
B
C
D
E
F
G
H
I
J
K
L
M
N
O
P
Q
R
S
T
U
V
W
X
Y
Z

> Have you ever eaten donkey? Little bit of rosemary, bit of thyme, bit of garlic, tenderise it, 170° for about six hours, it'll be lovely.

Nissan GT-R – too powerful for Jeremy's neck

Jamie Oliver

Cheery celebrity chef who detests school dinners and is also surprisingly good at rustling up a salad in the back of his camper van, even when The Stig is pounding it round the *Top Gear* test track.

Japan

Large country in East Asia that builds lots of cars: more than ten million every year, in fact. Believe it or not, thirty years ago, Japanese cars were considered a bit of a joke in Europe: slow, leaky rustboxes that would fall apart if you looked at them a bit funny. How times change.

Nowadays Japan builds some of the most reliable, trustworthy cars in the world. And some of the fastest cars in the world, too: just look at the Nissan GT-R and Lexus LFA!

Jay Kay

Lead singer of jazz-funk band Jamiroquai and the fastest celeb ever to lap the *Top Gear* test track in the Chevrolet Lacetti. Mr Kay also owns a rather excellent collection of exotic cars, including a Ferrari Enzo.

Jay Leno

Broad-chinned American talk show host with one of the very best collections of cars anywhere in the world.

> People ask, 'When are you going back on *Top Gear*? Are you going to beat Simon Cowell?' I don't care about the [beep] music now, I just gotta win it! Aargh!

JCB Dieselmax

British-built streamliner that, in 2006, set a land speed record for diesel cars when it hit 350mph at Bonneville Salt Flats. This broke the existing diesel record by over 100mph.

Jeep

Chrysler-owned American marque famous for building rugged 4x4s. The very first Jeeps were simple, no-frills four-wheel drives built for use by American soldiers during World War II. Since then, Jeeps have gained a little more luxury – not to mention roofs and doors. – but still maintain the go-anywhere spirit of the original military vehicles.

> What do you think about putting guns on F1 cars?

> I love the ideas you're coming up with. You've got a lot of time on your hands.

Jenson Button

British racing driver who competed in 112 F1 races before taking his first win in 2006. This win came a week after appearing as *Top Gear*'s Star In A Reasonably Priced Car for the first time. Coincidence? We think not. Button also won the F1 Drivers Championship in 2009, becoming the tenth Briton to do so…

Jensen Interceptor

Badly-built British GT car of the 1970s. According to Jeremy, the reason that no TV detective shows ever featured the Interceptor was because it was so unreliable that it would have broken down before the goodies could

ever catch any baddies. But now a British firm makes old-fashioned Interceptors with lots of fast, reliable modern bits underneath, making it the perfect car for a trio of crime-fighting, moustache-wearing *Top Gear* detectives. They're called… The Interceptors!

Jeremy Clarkson

Large human who resides in Chipping Norton and shouts loudly about cars. Jeremy is renowned for his considered, thoughtful approach to testing cars… no, hang on, that's not right, is it? What we meant to say was: Jeremy is renowned for his blunt, outspoken opinions and for offending nearly everyone in the world at one time or another. Jeremy's exact height is not known, as a ruler long enough to measure him has yet to be invented. Jeremy has never successfully mended a car.

Jet engine

Powerful engine commonly used on commercial aeroplanes and very good at destroying badly parked Nissan Sunnys…

Johnny Vegas

British comedian who, despite having not passed his driving test, still managed to lap the *Top Gear* test track in under two minutes in the Suzuki Liana.

Every single thing I do is rubbish.*

Jumper

James May's favourite item of clothing.

•*Said when building a Caterham kit car*

Kk

> This old airport . . . it's like a playground to me. There's not many places where you have such a great mix of dirt and tarmac, open spaces and nice obstacles.

Kei cars

Tiny vehicles built to strict Japanese regulations limiting size and engine power. In other words, they're tiny and weedy. Kei cars that have made it to the UK include the Daihatsu Copen and the Mitsubishi i.

Ken Block

American rally driver who does two things very well. One: make amazing Internet videos in which he slides rally cars with tyre-smoking precision around tricky obstacle courses. Two: scare James May by sliding rally cars with tyre-smoking precision around tricky obstacle courses.

Kerb weight

Car-speak for 'how heavy a car is'. Kerb weight is important because it is weight as much as power that affects how fast a car will go round a track: there's no point in giving a car a 500bhp V8 if it weighs the same as a small house and leans around corners like a sailboat in a storm. The lightest cars on the road, such as the Caterham R500, tip the scales at barely 500kg: the heaviest, such as the Maybach 62 and Bentley Brooklands, are nearer to 3000kg – that's three tonnes.

Kia

Korean manufacturer of *Top Gear*'s Reasonably Priced Cee-apostrophe-d and a bunch of other well-priced and thoroughly reliable cars. When you buy a new Kia, the company promises that nothing will go wrong with your car for SEVEN YEARS. If it does, they'll take it straight back and fix it. They must be pretty confident in how reliable their cars are, then…

Kia Cee'd

Top Gear's current Reasonably Priced Car. Confusing apostrophe.

Kilometres per hour

What the confusing French and Germans and Italians use instead of good old British miles per hour. One kilometre per hour equals precisely 0.6214 miles per hour, which means that 100kmph is just over 60mph.

A B C D E F G H I J K L M N O P Q R S T U V W X Y Z

It's alright, I've got it. Don't worry about the big heavy engine and the small guy holding it.

Kit car

Car sold as a big box of parts for assembly by the new owner. Kit cars tend to be small, lightweight sports cars – probably because it'd take the average DIYer several decades to assemble a giant SUV. As the boys discovered when they attempted to build a Caterham quicker than The Stig could drive from London up to Scotland, generally it's better to pay a qualified mechanic to put your car together…

Koenigsegg

Swedish maker of mad, bad supercars with an appetite for white-suited racing drivers. Lots of firms have attempted to join Ferrari and Lamborghini's Supercar Club in the last few years, but very few have succeeded. Koenigsegg has managed it by making cars that are scarier than spending an hour trapped in a lift with a hungry python with toothache.

Koenigsegg Agera

The successor to the Stig-devouring CCX, and even more mental. With a twin-turbo 940bhp V8 engine, the Agera will accelerate from 0-60mph in under three seconds and, claims Koenigsegg, it's capable of over 270mph flat-out. Only problem is, no one's been brave enough to test that claim out.

Jeremy Clarkson. It was Ms Scott Thomas's sophistication that made her the inspiration for *Top Gear*'s Cool Wall: Jeremy decided a car could only be considered 'Cool' if it would impress Kristin. When Kristen finally appeared as *Top Gear*'s Star In A Reasonably Priced Car, Jeremy could barely control himself.

Koenigsegg CCX

The car that tried to kill The Stig. *Top Gear*'s tame racing driver crashed the vicious CCX into a tyre wall trying to set a Power Lap in 2007, but after Koenigsegg fitted it with the '*Top Gear* wing', Stig took the CCX round the track in a blistering 1m17.6secs.

Kristin Scott Thomas

English actress famed for her appearances in *The English Patient* and *Four Weddings and a Funeral*, and the dream woman of Mr

KTM X-Bow

KTM is an Austrian company that builds motorbikes. So no surprise that its first attempt at a car – pronounced 'Cross-Bow' – is an open-air, extreme affair. The X-Bow has a turbocharged Audi engine, but absolutely no windscreen or roof: prepare to get wet if it rains…

L1

Laguna Seca

Scary American race track which is home to the truly terrifying 'Corkscrew' corner. As Jeremy discovered when he attempted to go round Laguna Seca in a Honda NSX as quickly as he could on a games console, it's much easier to take this corner in the safe virtual world than in real life.

> I do not have the skill to do that. I'm losing five, six seconds there.

Lamborghini

Bonkers Italian company that invented the very idea of a supercar. In 1966, Lamborghini introduced the beautiful Miura, the car that inspired every mad supercar since. But hadn't Ferrari, Jaguar and Bentley been building fast cars for years before 1966? Yes, but two things were different about the Miura. Firstly, it was the first mid-engined road car: in other words, its V12 engine was in front of the rear wheels but behind the driver. Secondly, the Miura didn't try to look subtle or sophisticated, but instead was designed to look as jaw-dropping and attention-grabbing as possible.

Lamborghini Aventador

Every big Lamborghini since the original 350GTV in 1963 used a

variation of the company's original V12 engine. The Aventador is the first Lambo to get an all-new V12 engine in almost fifty years, and what an engine it is: 6.5 litres and 691bhp of screaming V12 mayhem.

Lamborghini Gallardo

They call it the 'baby' Lambo, but don't be fooled: with a 560bhp 5.2-litre V10 engine and the ability to hit 60mph in just over three seconds, this is one baby you won't mess with.

A big V12 is its signature dish. It's what defines the car.

A
B
C
D
E
F
G
H
I
J
K
L
M
N
O
P
Q
R
S
T
U
V
W
X
Y
Z

Lamborghini Murcielago SV

Before replacing the Murcielago, Lamborghini sent it off with a final bonkers flourish: the huge-winged, hugely powerful 'Super Veloce'. Hammond thrashed it across the Abu Dhabi desert and was lost for words.

Lamborghini Reventon

Amazing hypercar based on the Murcielago and styled to look like a jet fighter. *Top Gear* likes jet fighters. The only real issue with the Reventon is how to pronounce it. According to Richard, it's pronounced 'Re-*v*en-Ton'. According to Jeremy, it's pronounced 'Re-*b*en-Ton'. We're still not sure which is right, so we'll pronounce it as 'the million-pound super-Lambo that looks like a stealth fighter' instead.

That noise! That glorious noise!

Lancia

Italian manufacturer that, according to Jeremy and Richard, has made more great cars than any other company. Seven, to be precise. Through the years, Lancia has pioneered masses of new technology: it was the first company to make a five-speed gearbox, the first company to make a V6 engine on a road car, and the first company to develop a monocoque. So why isn't it more famous? Erm, because Lancias always had a tendency to disintegrate into a large pile of rust and wires at the first sign of rain.

To show how reliable it is, I'm going to drive this 1982 HPE non-stop through the night on a rough rally stage.

WPY 514 Y

Oh no, look! I can't see through the flames!

Lancia Stratos

Beautiful, wedgy Italian sports car that won the World Rally Championship three times between 1974 and 1976. Buying a pristine Stratos today would cost you an arm and a leg, but you could always go for a replica **Hawk** (*see page 68*) instead. Or maybe not…

What a fantastic car!

Noisy, basic and uncomfortable, but also one of the toughest vehicles on the planet.

Le Mans

Town in northern France and location of the world's greatest endurance race. The 24 Hours of Le Mans has run since 1923, and sees drivers in a mighty array of racers and sports cars pound round the high-speed Circuit de la Sarthe non-stop for an entire day. In recent years, the 24 Hours of Le Mans has been dominated by Peugot and Audi diesel racers, which can cover over 3,000 miles in the course of the race…

Land Rover

If you close your eyes and picture a big, no-nonsense, mud-plugging 4x4, chances are it'll look a lot like a Land Rover. The first Land Rover was built after the Second World War as an alternative to the tractor, a vehicle in which farmers could trundle around their fields. Over the last six decades, Land Rovers have become more road-going and luxurious, the line-up now including posh SUVs like the Range Rover Evoque. But Land Rover hasn't forgotten its roots: it still makes cars capable of crawling up volcanoes and through rain forests: cars like the…

Land Rover Defender

The direct descendant of the original Land Rover from 1947.

> It is quite exciting when you're flying headfirst into a barrier!

Lewis Hamilton

British F1 driver currently racing for McLaren. In 2007, Lewis tackled the *Top Gear* test track in the Suzuki Liana, posting a blistering time of 1m44.7 on a wet and oily track. Jeremy likes to think it was his fatherly advice that helped Lewis win the F1 World Championship the following year!

Lexus

Toyota's luxury division, responsible for making posh but very, very dull cars for people who enjoy golf and wearing suits. Lexus cars had a reputation for being more boring than watching a chess championship in slow motion… but then they went and built the insane LFA, a 552bhp V10 supercar that Richard discovered was fast and agile enough to evade… alien spaceships.

Lillehammer without the snow: just a big hill.

Liberal Democrats

The fastest British political party, according to important research conducted by *Top Gear* back in 2003.

Lightning

Spark of atmospheric electricity, capable of reaching speeds of 140,000mph and temperatures of 30,000°C. Though the odds of getting struck by lightning are literally one in a million, the results can be deadly. However, as Richard discovered when he was zapped by eight thousand volts of electricity in a German laboratory, you might just survive a lightning strike if you're inside a VW Golf!

Lillehammer

Snowy Norwegian town that held the proper Winter Olympics in 1994, and the *Top Gear* Winter Olympics in 2006.

I hate snow.

Ooh that's scary. My hands are buzzing!

Limousine

A luxurious car designed to transport important people from one important place to another important place. In order to give its important passengers the most comfortable journey, limousines are often lengthened – or

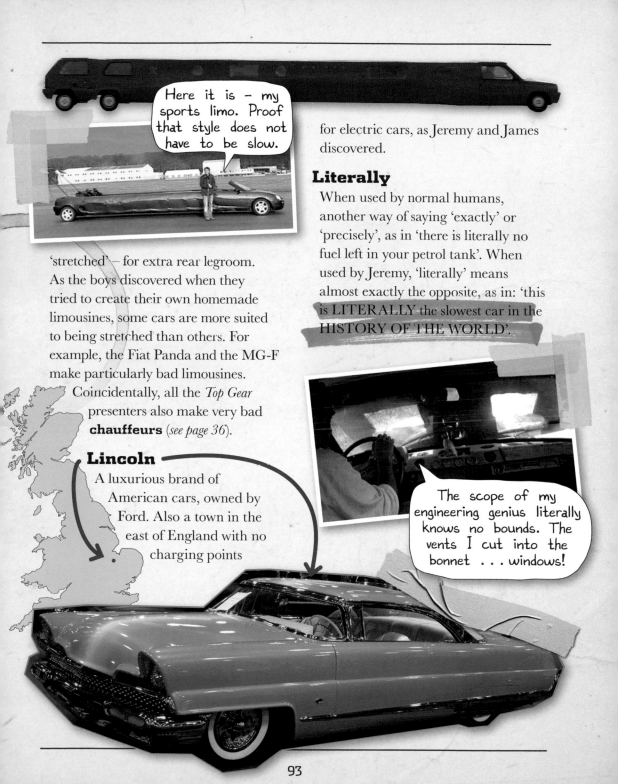

Here it is — my sports limo. Proof that style does not have to be slow.

'stretched' – for extra rear legroom. As the boys discovered when they tried to create their own homemade limousines, some cars are more suited to being stretched than others. For example, the Fiat Panda and the MG-F make particularly bad limousines.

Coincidentally, all the *Top Gear* presenters also make very bad **chauffeurs** (*see page 36*).

Lincoln

A luxurious brand of American cars, owned by Ford. Also a town in the east of England with no charging points

for electric cars, as Jeremy and James discovered.

Literally

When used by normal humans, another way of saying 'exactly' or 'precisely', as in 'there is literally no fuel left in your petrol tank'. When used by Jeremy, 'literally' means almost exactly the opposite, as in: 'this is LITERALLY the slowest car in the HISTORY OF THE WORLD'.

The scope of my engineering genius literally knows no bounds. The vents I cut into the bonnet . . . windows!

Lorry

Huge boxy vehicles designed to transport large amounts of stuff and responsible for enormous lines of traffic on Britain's A-roads. Many people think that lorry driving is an easy job involving a few hours behind the wheel followed by a very long lunch of eggs, sausage and beans, but as Jeremy, James and Richard discovered, it's not as easy as it looks. Jeremy, especially, will confirm that driving a lorry is not only complicated, but will often end in quite serious injury…

This lorry driving is quite a lot harder than I thought. The gear lever's gone up my . . .

Oof! Argh! Urgh! Ow, this actually really hurts.

Lotus

Norfolk-based firm that makes heavy, slow, luxurious cars. Hang on, that's not right, is it? We mean: British firm that makes very light, very unluxurious cars that drive in a way that means you really ought to empty all the loose change from your pockets before getting into the driver's seat. Lotus was founded by **Colin Chapman** (*see page 40*) in the 1950s and immediately went about dominating F1, winning seven championships between 1963 and 1978. But Lotus isn't only good at building race cars: it also makes some of the best-driving sports cars on the planet, including the…

AU09 AKZ

Even by supercar standards, this is fantastic. Properly, properly fantastic.

or (b) so super-rich that you can afford to buy your own F1 team. So what happens if you're a normal human but want to experience the thrill of an F1 car? That's where the Lotus T125 comes in. With 640bhp and weighing less than a ballet shoe, this is one of the most extreme racing cars ever made, but it's one that can be bought by the general public. Just a couple of problems: one, it costs over a million pounds and two, as Jeremy found out, it requires a total recalibration of your brain in order to drive...

Lotus Exige

A hardcore track car that's so light and so nimble, it'll evade missile lock from an Apache helicopter!

Lotus T125

The problem with driving an F1 car is that you... can't. Not unless you're (a) such a super-talented driver that McLaren decides to ditch Lewis Hamilton and employ you instead

> Have you seen a Fiat? A small, black-and-white Fiat?

Lucca

Historic walled city in north-west Italy that's very difficult to escape from. Especially if you're trapped in the middle in a hot hatch and you're called Richard Hammond.

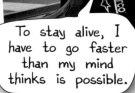

> To stay alive, I have to go faster than my mind thinks is possible.

Mm

"Only my Opel remained trouble-free . . ."

Makgadikadi

Huge flat salt pan in Botswana, formed when a giant lake dried out thousands of years ago. When the boys attempted to cross the fearsome Makgadikadi (pronounced My-Caddy-Caddy) on their Botswana adventure, they discovered that it's (a) very empty and (b) very easy to get stuck in…

Marauder

South Africa doesn't build many cars. But when it does, it doesn't mess around. The Marauder is an armoured vehicle so tough that it can smash straight through brick walls, flatten cars… or survive an explosion from a roadside bomb! Just one tiny problem: it costs £300,000, which is an awful lot of pocket money.

Maserati

Italian maker of beautiful, luxurious cars, founded way back in 1914. Though closely related to Ferrari – they're both owned by Fiat and share engines and technology – Maserati has always built more laid-back, easy-going cars than its Italian neighbour. With one notable exception, the…

Oh, that's so quick! What a bonkers car! Holey moley, what a fun machine!

Maserati MC12

Insane road-legal race car based on the equally crazy Ferrari Enzo. With a 620bhp V12 engine and carbon fibre bodywork, the MC12 can get from 0-60mph in 3.6 seconds and does 205mph flat out.

Mastretta MXT

A sports car entirely designed and built in Mexico. Which is good. The Mastretta MXT is very nice. That is all.

Maybach

What car should you buy if (a) you want something incredibly expensive, large and luxurious but (b) you don't want a Rolls-Royce and you'd prefer something German? Well, you should probably buy a Rolls-Royce, as it's owned by BMW, but Mercedes thought you might prefer to buy a Maybach, its own attempt to part billionaires from their cash. Unfortunately, the super-size and super-priced Maybach didn't prove very popular with buyers, and died out in 2012.

Mazda

Japanese manufacturer responsible for some good sensible family cars, but also a couple of truly lovely sports cars in the shape of the rotary-engined RX-8 – which has sadly been killed off in the last couple of years – and the...

Mazda MX-5

Lovely little rear-wheel drive coupe, as modified by Jeremy on the boys' Middle East adventure. The MX-5 is a lightweight, delicately balanced sports car that is not improved by the

What I've done here is create a car of many colours. I am Joseph!

addition of extra rear wheels or a 'Technicolour Dreamcoat' paintjob…

McLaren

British race team and one of the most successful F1 outfits of all time, winning (at last count) eight constructors championships and twelve drivers championships. Despite competing continuously in Formula One since 1966 (the year England won the football World Cup, don't forget), McLaren has still found time to cook up a couple of the most amazing road-going supercars in history…

McLaren F1

First produced in 1993, the 240mph F1 was a futuristic three-seater supercar that, for thirteen years, held the title of 'world's fastest car' until it was beaten by the Koenigsegg CCR in 2005. With a 6.1-litre V12 and astonishing handling, the McLaren F1 remains the fastest non-turbocharged car in history.

Lewis Hamilton in his McLaren in Malaysia, 2009.

There's something missing. Something that can't be measured. Something you can't really put your finger on. There's no . . . zing.

McLaren MP4-12C

Twin-turbo 591bhp supercar that's cleverer than an especially clever astrophysicist... but somehow not quite as exciting as the Ferrari 458.

Mercedes Benz

German manufacturer rather like a librarian who's the lead singer of a death-metal band. Confused? Let us explain. Most of the time, Mercedes makes quiet, respectable family cars for quiet, respectable sorts – a librarian quietly filing books, if you will. But, every now and again, Mercedes lets its hair down and creates a mad, tyre-melting, ear-splitting, V8-powered slice of madness like the SLS AMG or SL Black Series, cars that'll scare the pants off you and melt your eardrums. See? It's a death-metal-band-librarian. Told you.

Mercedes SLS AMG

Roaring V12 supercar with amazing old-fashioned 'gullwing' doors, just like the original Mercedes 300SL of 1954.

Mercedes-Benz Grosser

Huge old limousine originally used to transport royalty and dictators in leathery luxury. When it was introduced in 1963, the Grosser was the most expensive car in the world. Nowadays you can pick up a Grosser for a mere £25,000. But what sort of human would buy a 1960s car that weighs nearly three tonnes and has the approximate dimensions of a three-bedroom bungalow? Ah…

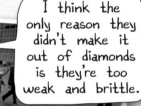

> I think the only reason they didn't make it out of diamonds is they're too weak and brittle.

won his first F1 drivers championship in 1994 and went on to take a further six crowns, his last coming in 2004. In 2006, Schumacher announced his retirement from F1, and in 2009 was 'unmasked' on the poxy BBC2 motoring show '*Top Gear*' as tame racing driver 'The Stig'. Later that year he returned to Formula One, leading many to wonder how he'd possibly have time to fit in racing around the world… and test out cars around the *Top Gear* circuit. It remains a mystery to this day.

Michael Schumacher

The most successful F1 racing driver of all time. Born in Germany in 1969, Schumacher won every karting championship in Europe and in 1991 made his Formula One debut. It was the beginning of an era: Schumacher

It is a magnificent achievement. So what does it have to do with our big, heavy, thirsty, expensive cars?

This is a supercar, like that is a superbridge.

Millau Viaduct

Amazing lump of engineering found in southern France, and crossed by the *TG* boys on their big French supercar road trip in 2005. The Millau is the tallest bridge in the world, with its highest mast standing a towering 343 metres high. That's twenty metres taller than the Eiffel Tower.

Mini

Back in 1959, the British Motor Corporation introduced a tiny, affordable car. It was revolutionary. Unlike almost any other car of the day, it was front-wheel drive, lightweight, and its engine sat sideways under the bonnet rather than front-to-back. It was called the Mini, and it was one of the most iconic British cars of all time. The original Mini continued in production until 2000, selling over five million models around the world. At the turn of the century, BMW bought the rights to the Mini name, and in

don't matter in the world of *Top Gear*. Most of Mitsubishi's cars are very important if you're a farmer or attempting to deliver medicine to the middle of the African rain forest, as they're indestructible and capable of getting just about anywhere. However, they're not so entertaining around the *Top Gear* track. Apart from the...

Mitsubishi Lancer Evo

Bonkers four-wheel drive saloon car that will match most supercars around a race track, and defeat most supercars on a wiggly back-road. It isn't pretty, and it won't ever live on the right-hand side of *Top Gear*'s Cool Wall, but the turbocharged, rally-ready Evo is one of the most effective ways of getting down a road quickly.

2001 introduced the 'new' Mini, which was built in Britain and became an immediate hit.

Mitsubishi

Japanese maker of (a) big gruff 4x4s (b) insane four-wheel drive rally cars and (c) ships and beer and paper and plastic and electronics and lots of other things that

It is genuinely incredible. There is no car that handles like this one.

Its looks are based on a fish, a snake and Pamela Anderson's mouth.

streets with a large watery sea to land in if you get things wrong. As the boys discovered when they tackled Monaco's F1 circuit in their trio of hot hatches, you need a lot of bravery to put in a decent lap time here…

Monocoque

Pronounced 'mono-cock' (don't you dare laugh) and meaning 'single-shell', monocoque describes the way in which most modern cars are constructed. Once upon a time, vehicles were built with their wheels, suspension and engine sitting on a ladder-like frame, with the bodywork plonked on top after. But with a monocoque chassis,

Mitsuoka

Strange Japanese firm responsible for some of the ugliest vehicles ever created. When James May tested out the Orochi and the Galue in Japan, he was impressed with their comfortable ride and interior space… but not quite so impressed with their guppy-fish looks!

Monaco

Tiny city in South France that, for Historical Reasons, is also an independent country. More importantly, it's also host to the Monaco Grand Prix, a bum-clenching race around narrow city

I am out of my depth to a degree I have never before experienced.

The carbon-fibre monococque from the Lambo Aventador.

it's the entire 'shell' of the car – the doors, the roof and the stuff underneath – that gives the structure its strength. Confused? Imagine this: a traditional car is constructed like a shoebox (the body) sitting on top of a ladder (the chassis). A monocoque is more like a chicken's egg.

Morgan

British maker of odd, old-fashioned cars that Hammond likes very much. Morgan started out in 1911 with three-wheelers largely constructed of wood… but has changed dramatically over the years. Nowadays it builds three- AND four-wheelers out of wood.

Morgan 3-Wheeler

Yes, Morgan really does make a 3-Wheeler. In the twenty first century. It has a noisy motorbike engine. It has one wheel too few. It's… quite cool, isn't it?

Lightness is good. You could pick this up and put it in your pocket.

longer beeps. So the letter 'S' is dot-dot-dot, and the letter 'O' is dash-dash-dash. The Stig enjoys listening to Morse Code while driving.

Motorbike

Two-wheeled motorized vehicle usually driven by men wearing a large quantity of cow-skin. Despite the motorbike's obvious issues – the fact that you get very wet when it rains, and very dead when you crash – both James and Richard seem to be quite keen on them.

Morris Marina

Rubbish car built in Britain in the 1970s and destroyed in great numbers by *Top Gear*. The Morris Marina Owners Club gets very upset that *Top Gear* has exterminated so many of these horrible old cars, but really, aren't we doing them a favour?

Morse Code

Method of communication in which letters are spelled out using a combination of 'dots' and 'dashes' – or shorter and

Motorhome racing

Traditionally, amateur racers go off for a weekend of racing with a motorhome to sleep in, and a race car hitched behind for when they reach the track. Richard figured he could save a lot of time and effort by combining the two into the sport of motorhome racing. Motorhome racing turned out to be quite a crashy sort of contact sport. Despite its entertainment value, it doesn't seem to have replaced Formula One as the world's favourite motorsport.

Mum

British slang word for a female parent. Mums are very good at lots of things: making sure you don't go to school with jam smeared all over your face, remembering where you've put your PE kit… but most of all, they're very good at reviewing small cars. At least, they are if they're the mums of *Top Gear* presenters!

The rules are simple: fifteen laps and no body contact.

This is Mrs May, who drives a Seat Arosa. She's been done for speeding twice, which is two times more than James.

I think the no-contact rule needs a bit of a tweak.

Nn

NASCAR

Abbreviation for National Association of Stock Car Auto Racing, and the most popular motorsport in the US of A. Because NASCAR racers are big, basic-looking machines that run on simple oval circuits, NASCAR is often dismissed by F1 fans as nothing more than 'turning left'. However, as Richard discovered when he visited Texas Speedway, there's a lot more to NASCAR than that...

Neck

Body part connecting head to shoulders, as injured by Jeremy when testing the fearsome Nissan GT-R at Fuji Speedway.

News, The

Section of *Top Gear* telly in which Jeremy, James and Richard are supposed to discuss brand-new cars

> It's not just a big loop, it's complex. It's three-dimensional. And I'm wrestling my way round it in a huge shouty dragon!

and recent developments in the world of motoring. However, The News usually descends into a lot of silly name-calling and jokes that result in many letters of complaint.

Nigel Mansell

Once-moustachioed British racing driver who won the F1 driver's championship back in 1992. In 2005, Mansell took the Suzuki Liana round the TG track in a time of 1m44.6, the fastest-ever Liana lap at the time.

Nissan

Car maker once known as Datsun, and one of the biggest manufacturers in Japan. Nissan makes a weird and wonderful array of cars, from the oddball Cube to the insanely-fast GT-R to the all-electric Leaf – and that's not all: it also owns the luxury car maker Infiniti too…

Nissan Cube

Boxy, wonky city car that was once the best-selling car in Japan. Jeremy described it as 'absolutely hopeless'.

> The square simply isn't a frightening shape.

Nissan GT-R

Twin-turbo, four-wheel drive sports car that'll do 0-60mph in under three seconds and will thrash Ferraris, Lamborghinis and Paganis in real world, real road driving. And, unbelievably, it costs just £70,000.

Nissan Leaf

All-electric family car driven to Lincoln by Jeremy and James. Some say electric cars like the Leaf will save the planet. But you'll have to find somewhere to charge it up…

> This is the future of motoring. This is what's going to beome of you all.

A B C D E F G H I J K L M **N** O P Q R S T U V W X Y Z

I can't do any more. I've done enough. I just can't take it.

Hi, this is the car. Please talk to me.

Nissan Micra C+C

Ugly little convertible often painted pink. Oh, and 'the most embarrassing car in human history', according to Richard Hammond.

Nissan Sunny

Rubbish old Japanese car that cannot withstand attack by a dragster jet engine.

Nissank

Amphibious vehicle created by renowned inventor Jeremy Clarkson. Based on a Nissan pick-up truck, the Nissank successfully transported Jeremy, James and Richard across the English Channel in 2007, but failed to break Richard Branson's record for the fastest journey from England to France in an amphibious vehicle.

Noble M600

British supercar built in a shed in Leicestershire around a Volvo engine.

Doesn't sound very promising? Think again. With its twin turbochargers turned up to full boost, the M600 will make 650bhp, do 0-60mph in three seconds and 225mph flat out. But, as Hammond discovered on the boys' Italian supercar road trip, it may occasionally break down, leaving you at the mercy of the Italian version of the AA…

North Pole

The most northerly point on Earth. Simple, right? Not quite. See, unlike the South Pole, which sits on a solid, frozen lump of land, the North Pole is in the middle of the Arctic ocean, a vast expanse of drifting ice floes that refuse to stay still. So, because you can't stick a flag in the ground to mark the spot, the North Pole is found by following a compass until you can go no further north. But even that's not quite straightforward, as the Earth has a pesky tendency to 'wobble' magnetically around, moving the North Pole by a few miles each decade. This makes it very difficult to establish exactly *where* the North Pole is: just one of the challenges that Jeremy and James faced when they tried to drive a Hilux to the North Pole in 2007. Some of the other issues they encountered were (a) the extreme cold, (b) the fact that Hammond was chasing them down on a dog sled and (c) trying to go to the loo without freezing their extremities off!

Clarkson! You insufferable oaf, I'm on the throne!

Ready? Ready . . . wait for it . . . Yes! Yeeaahh!!

111

Norway

Chilly Scandinavian country that, to *Top Gear*'s knowledge, has never built a decent car. Norway is included in the *Stigtionary* solely because, as Jeremy discovered, it is quicker to get to from Britain in a McLaren-Mercedes SLR than it is on a ferry. Oh, and it's a good place to hold Car Winter Olympics, too...

I'm here and have been for some time.

Norwich Airport

International airport located in the east of England. If you happen to drift into Norwich Airport's air space in a caravan airship, you will end up in a lot of trouble.

If she does this, nuns ROCK!

Nun

A woman who has taken vows to live a spiritual life. Having dedicated their existence to peace, charity and prayer, you wouldn't expect nuns to be much good at driving monster trucks over a line of rusty cars. However, as Richard (and Sister Wendy) proved, they're actually surprisingly good at it.

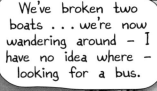

We've broken two boats . . . we're now wandering around – I have no idea where – looking for a bus.

Nürburgring

Race track in western Germany christened 'The Green Hell' by Jackie Stewart. Why? Because it's terrifying. The Nürburgring consists of fourteen miles and seventy-three corners of sheer adrenaline: a twisting, high-

(Is that Sabine Schmitz in the Ring-Taxi?)

speed circuit on which cars can reach 200mph as they whizz past trees and barriers: no friendly gravel traps or tyre walls here. The scariest thing about the Nürburgring is that literally ANYONE can drive it. Because it's technically a public road, any member of the public can turn up in their creaky road car, pay a few Euros and scare themselves silly. Or crash. The fastest ever lap of the Nürburgring was by bonkers German race driver Stefan Bellof back in 1983, who went round in a time of just 6m26s in his Porsche 956 racer. As you might have noticed, James May hates the Nürburgring. He believes it's the reason that all modern sports cars ride like their suspension is made of granite.

Car makers become obsessed with making their cars go round this irrelevant historical German racetrack as fast as possible, without realising that they're ruining the car for those of us who live in the real world.

in the USA has an octane rating (RON) of 91, while British unleaded petrol is usually around 95 RON. F1 fuel is about 102 RON, while the fuel put in dragsters is so potent it can't even be measured on the normal octane scale.

Oliver

Top Gear doesn't believe in naming cars. Giving your car a name is as ridiculous as calling your toaster 'Gary' or your fridge 'Hortensia'. Which is why it came as a bit of a surprise when Richard christened the 1963 Opel Kadett that valiantly carried him across Botswana. It came as even more of a surprise that he christened it 'Oliver'. When the boys had finished filming in Botswana, Richard had Oliver flown back to the UK, and the two now live happily

Octane

Measurement of how much 'bang' there is in fuel. Petrol with a higher octane rating will allow a car to produce more power. Standard petrol

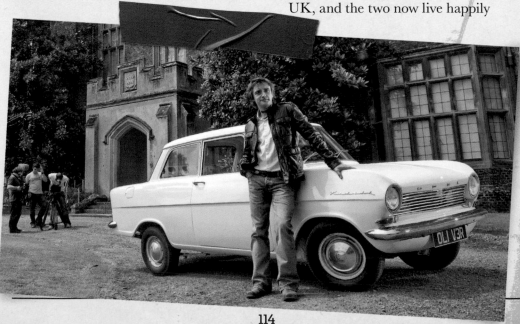

together in the Welsh countryside.

Oompah band
Traditional German musical ensemble that can fit inside a budget sports saloon. At a squeeze.

Overfinch
British company that specialises in 'enhancing' Range Rovers. Mainly with posh glasses, drinks cabinets and gun racks.

Oversteer
You know all those Power Tests where Jeremy slides something hideously powerful and rear-wheel drive round the *Top Gear* track in a big cloud of tyre-smoke? That's oversteer. Well, mainly. Oversteer is the technical term for the tendency of the rear wheels of a car to try and 'overtake' the front wheels in a corner. In the hands of a skilled driver, this can end up with the car going 'sideways' and drifting in a spectacular, controlled slide. In the hands of most people, this ends up with the car off the side of the track, facing the wrong way.

The cost of all this is . . . £139,000.

Pp

Pagani

Bonkers Italian car company founded in 1992 by a former Lamborghini engineer. Dozens of upstart supercar makers have attempted to muscle into Ferrari and Lamborghini territory in the last couple of decades, but Pagani is one of the very few to succeed. How did it manage it? By making cars madder than, erm, Jeremy Clarkson after he's been forced to spend a week driving a Ssangyong. The company's first car was the astonishing…

Pagani Zonda

Beautiful, swoopy hypercar with a Mercedes AMG V12 engine in the middle. The Zonda started life in 1999 with the C12 model producing around 400bhp, and ended in 2011 with the insane 'Zonda R' racer, which made 740bhp and broke the Nürburgring lap record for production-based race cars.

The acceleration is so brutal! I think my eyes have moved round the side of my head, like a pigeon's!

Pamplona Bull Run

Spanish festival where hundreds of insane locals are chased through narrow city streets by a herd of fearsome, razor-horned bulls. The Pamplona Bull Run is incredibly dangerous: each year, dozens of people are gored by the bulls' horns, and even deaths are not unusual. So, when *Top Gear*

> And we're running! This is terrifying – people are just tearing to get away!

> Ooh, this looks good – Yes, yess!!

needed someone to run with the bulls before testing out the Lamborghini Murcielago Roadster, there was only one man daft enough for the job: Hammond.

Parachuting

Method of falling from a plane to the ground without ending up as a small pile of splattered human. But is it possible to parachute from a plane into a car moving at 50mph? It's a question that no one had ever asked until *Top Gear* came along. And it turns out the answer is: yes, it is possible to parachute from a plane into a car, but it's really quite difficult. And probably not a very good idea.

A
B
C
D
E
F
G
H
I
J
K
L
M
N
O
P
Q
R
S
T
U
V
W
X
Y
Z

> There they are! They look as though they've nicked something.

Parkour

Acrobatic sport that combines free-running and acrobatics. Traceurs – as those who do parkour are known – use a combination of flipping, jumping, climbing and sprinting to get around cities as quickly as possible. It's not only athletic and spectacular, but also – as James discovered when he raced two parkour runners across Liverpool in a Peugeot 207 GTi – a quicker way to cross a city than by car.

Peel P50

The smallest car ever made. First built in 1962, the P50 was a three-wheeled microcar less than a metre and a half long, a metre wide and weighing just 60kg. It was powered by a 49cc engine producing only four horsepower, and had a top speed of 38mph. You might think, therefore, that the Peel P50 was useless, tiny, slow and dangerous. But as Jeremy proved, it's actually brilliant: the Peel is so tiny that you can literally drive it into the office.

Pendine Sands

Huge flat beach in South Wales that has hosted speed record attempts for over a century. Pendine's smooth sand and seven-mile length have always made it a good place to carry out top-speed runs. Way back in 1924, English daredevil Malcolm Campbell set a land speed record when he hit 146mph in his 'Bluebird' racer. Back in 2004, *Top Gear* tested out three rear-wheel drive sports cars – the BMW 645Ci, Jaguar XK-R and Porsche 911 – on the Pendine beach, and found it to be an excellent place to practise big sandy powerslides.

People Carrier

A big van designed to carry humans, also known as an MPV (multi-purpose vehicle). People carriers have generally been regarded as some of the most boring vehicles on the planet, as they're more bothered with transporting as many people as possible than sharp-edged sporty handling. So Hammond decided to make them a little more interesting by inventing the

So here we are. All three cars together on this enormous playground.

We think this sport has great promise. It'll be cheap, exciting and it's open to minicabbers and dads. It should also be a good laugh.

sport of Historic People Carrier Racing. It ended with a lot of understeer. And crashing...

Petrol

The liquid that makes the world go round. Not literally. That's gravity and physics and stuff. But petrol is responsible for almost all the speed and noise that *Top Gear* loves so much. Like diesel, petrol is distilled from crude oil, but is more explosive, explaining why it's used in most racers and supercars. The amount of 'bang' in petrol is measured by its **octane** (*see page 114*) rating: in short, the higher the rating, the faster it'll go.

Peugeot

French car company that, back in the 1980s, made a bunch of brilliant hot hatches like the 205 GTi, but has spent most of the last two decades churning out boring family cars with electrical systems less reliable than James's map-reading skills. Since 2007, Peugeot has been desperately trying to defeat Audi in the 24 Hours of Le Mans, but has only succeeded once, in 2009. Its attempt at racing might not have been a total success, but recent arrivals like the curvy-roofed RCZ suggest that Peugeot might finally have remembered how to build decent road cars.

Peugeot iOn

Dinky all-electric car that, as Jeremy and James discovered, cannot get to the seaside and back without requiring a recharge.

Batteries . . . batteries are rubbish.

Piano

Large musical instrument played by James May and frequently destroyed by immature television programme *Top Gear*. So far we've seen a piano ruined after being reversed into by a lorry, and another falling on top of a Morris Marina. What fate shall befall the next one?

Pick-up truck

Vehicle with a big open cargo deck at the rear. In Britain, pick-up trucks are traditionally used by builders to transport bricks, lumps of wood and so forth. In America, pick-up trucks are traditionally used to transport whatever animal the driver has just shot. *Top Gear*'s favourite pick-up truck, of course, is the indestructible **Toyota Hilux.**

Pierre Henri Raphanel

Bugatti test driver who took the Bugatti Veyron Super Sports to a record breaking 268mph just a few minutes after James May had set a new record of 257mph. This means that Raphanel is responsible for James May holding a rather unwanted world record: the man who held a land speed record for the shortest time.

Sorry, James!

Right. We've lost. Let's go home.

So the pillars to either side of the windscreen are the A-pillars, while the ones between the front and rear windows are the B-pillars, and so on…

Pigeon

Small domestic bird often kept for its homing instincts. As *Top Gear* proved, a well-trained homing pigeon is both faster and better at navigating than James May in a Ford SportKa. Then again, most things are faster and better at navigating than James May…

Pillar

Not the big columns that stand at the front of old-fashioned buildings, but the bits of a car that hold the roof on the body. Pillars are the technical name for the vertical bits of metal between a car's windows, and are named alphabetically.

Porsche

German manufacturer of brilliant sports cars. Established in 1931, Porsche quickly developed a reputation for making not only fast road cars but also brilliant racers, too: it has won the 24 Hours of Le Mans sixteen times, more than any other manufacturer. Porsche has

You only have to drive one of these things for five minutes to understand why it's SO good.

sometimes been criticised for making cars that all look the same, but this seems a bit unfair: OK, the 911 and Cayman might look similar, but the Cayenne looks nothing like either of them. It looks like a hippo…

Porsche 911

Rear-engined sports car originally based on the VW Beetle and first built in 1967. The 911 has always divided opinion among the *Top Gear* boys: James and Richard believe it is the ultimate evolution of the sports car and a thing of engineering wonder, while Jeremy believes it is a jumped-up Beetle with the engine at the wrong end…

That is a wretched, awful miserable, spluttering, puttering, slow, noisy, ugly piece of hateful misery and the worst attempt at a people's car the world has ever suffered, but –

– from it evolved this, the acknowledged finest driver's car and ultimate automotive precision tool that mankind has ever created.

Porsche Boxster Spyder

Tent-roofed sports car that, as James May discovered, is completely useless in the event of a sudden rainstorm…

> The 959 came with a million things we'd never seen before.

Porsche 959

1980s supercar tested by Hammond against the Ferrari F40. Which one would he want? Both, please!

Porsche Cayenne

"I have seen more attractive gangrenous wounds than this," gasped Jeremy when he tested Porsche's big

> So it's big, fast and stunning to drive. But none of that is important.

SUV. Despite its astonishing performance both on- and off-road, he simply couldn't get over its hideous looks...

Porsche Cayman

Dinky mid-engined coupé that Jeremy refers to as the 'Coxster'. Because it's a coupé Boxster, obviously...

Porsche Panamera

Rapid four-door saloon that can't get from the Isles of Scilly to the top of Scotland quite as quickly as a letter delivered by the Royal Mail.

I'm struggling to think of anyone who will look at the Coxster and think, 'Yes. That is a masterpiece.'

It's bonkers: it's massive, it does things a supercar does, only it has four doors.

Power

Technically, power is the rate at which energy is transferred or transformed. In *Top Gear* World, power is what makes cars go fast. The standard power measurement for cars is 'horsepower', as it originally referred to the amount of power created by a horse turning a mill wheel. That means that the Bugatti Veyron has more power than a thousand horses! In order to sound like Jeremy Clarkson, it's important to pronounce power with at least ten extra 'R's at the end, like this:

POWERRRRRRRRRRR!

Prodrive P2

Four-wheel drive British sports car with buckets of rally technology on-board. The Prodrive P2 can corner so hard that it makes Jeremy feel deeply nauseous. This would have been an excellent way to ensure some peace and quiet in the *Top Gear* office, but unfortunately the P2 never went into production. Pity...

Public Transport

How people who don't use cars get around. Public transport can include trains, buses, tubes and even boats, none of which are as good as an Aston Martin. Or a Ferrari. When The Stig attempted to get across London by public transport – in a race against Hammond on a bike, James in a car and Jeremy on a boat – he found it entirely bemusing. Then again, he finds most things that aren't cars bemusing...

Qq

Quattroporte

Sounds exotic, doesn't it? You might think Quattroporte – Maserati's name for its big, beautiful saloon – means something glamorous like 'speed' or 'passion'. But you'd be wrong. In fact, it means 'four-door' in Italian. 'Quattro' is four, 'porte' is door. Not quite so exotic now, is it? But when a car looks – and sounds – as good as this, who cares if its name is a bit boring?

Oh, my word! Yeahh! I'm in a four-door saloon, but it sounds magnificent – it's just got so much style!

A B C D E F G H I J K L M N O P **Q** R S T U V W X Y Z

Rr

Radio-control cars

Toy radio-control cars are great, but *Top Gear* decided they were a bit small. And safe. So James and Richard – with the help of some super-clever boffins – set out to discover if you could drive full-sized cars around a quarry… using radio control. The results were muddy, crashy and – for important scientific reasons – resulted in the destruction of many caravans.

Range Rover Evoque

Posh little SUV made by Land Rover. Despite being aimed at mud-avoiding city types, the Evoque is actually a proper off-road machine, as James discovered when he thrashed it across the Nevada desert.

This is weird!

Not very easy, this.

It's the perfect place to find out if the new Evoque is a proper Range Rover, or just a big designer girl's blouse.

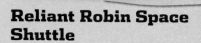

Rear-wheel drive

Type of car in which the engine drives the back wheels only. Most fast cars are rear-wheel drive (though an increasing number are moving to four-wheel drive) because this layout usually provides better balance, acceleration and handling. And, most importantly, it's the best configuration for doing big smoky powerslides.

Reliant Robin

British three-wheeler that's very cheap to tax because it technically qualifies as a motorcycle. Unfortunately the Reliant Robin shares another quality with motorcycles: falling over. A lot. In fact, if you drive like Jeremy Clarkson, you will find that the Reliant Robin falls over every time you go round a corner. If this happens, you'd better hope there's a friendly Yorkshireman on hand to turn you the right way up...

Reliant Robin Space Shuttle

Launching ANYTHING into space is a challenge far beyond *Top Gear's* engineering abilities. But launching a space shuttle – a vehicle designed not only to blast out of the atmosphere, but then also return safely to Earth – is tougher than trying to tie your shoelaces using a pair of chopsticks. James and Richard decided a Reliant Robin would be the best car to transform into a space shuttle, on account of it being, erm, a bit pointy at the front. They strapped eight tonnes of rocket power to the back, pressed the big red button and... well, things didn't go quite to plan...

J
K
L
M
N
O
P
Q
R
S
T
U
V
W
X
Y
Z

Excuse me, do you think you could push me back on my wheels?

Renault

French maker of quirky family cars and very good hot hatches. Renault was actually founded in the 19th century, but didn't really do anything interesting until 1980, when it launched the brilliant, boxy, mid-engined Renault 5 Turbo, which was the maddest fast hatchback of its day and pretty good at rallying too. Since then, Renault has made some of *Top Gear*'s very favourite hot hatches, including the buzzy Clio 200 driven by James around Monaco. Renault's other speciality is weird, big cars like the…

Renault Avantime

Quirky people-carrier that, no matter how many wings you stick to it, cannot get round the *Top Gear* test track as fast as a Mitsubishi Evo.

Renault Clio V6

Mad French hot hatch that had its engine BEHIND the front seats rather than in the usual location under the bonnet. This meant that it was (a) very entertaining but (b) rather prone to **oversteering** (*see page 115*) and then **crashing** (*see page 43*). Even so, Jeremy described it as more fun

visit a safari park. Or drive at speeds over 20mph. Or take it through a car wash…

Renault R25

The F1 car driven very badly round Silverstone by Hammond. In the hands of Spanish racer Fernando Alonso, the R25 won the F1 drivers and constructors title in 2005. In the hands of Hammond, it would win nothing at all…

> See, from a distance, it looks quite . . . this isn't its best side.

> Please can we go?

> I'M WET NOW!!

than 'watching the entire French air force crash into a fireworks factory'…

Renault Espace

Huge people carrier that, as the boys discovered, can also be made into an excellent seven-seater convertible. Excellent, that is, unless you're planning to

> I can't think fast enough, more than anything else.

Renault Twingo

Tiny French city car that can fit an entire Ross Kemp in its boot and drive upside down in a tunnel, but isn't very good at ice hockey.

Rental cars

Hired vehicles – often from a foreign airport – that will usually be battered, slow, and previously inhabited by someone with terrible hygiene problems. For this reason, Jeremy, James and Richard went to America to find out whether you could buy a second-hand car for less than the price of renting one. They discovered that (a) yes, you could save money by buying a second-hand car rather than renting

Bit of a squeeze, but quite comfy.

Roadkill

An animal that has been struck and killed by a car. Roadkill is a sad loss of animal life, but it's also – as *Top Gear* discovered in America – a useful source of food. How useful rather depends on what sort of animal has been killed: there's not much meat on a squirrel, but if you happen to find a cow that's been hit by a truck, you'll be feasting for weeks…

Roadworks

If you've ever sat in a traffic jam because half the road has been coned off to allow for 'emergency' repairs, you'll know what a pain in the bottom roadworks can be. *Top Gear* thought the biggest problem with roadworks is that they take too long, and decided to discover if repairs that would normally take a week could be done in twenty-four hours. Jeremy, James and Richard found out that it was indeed possible – but not without making a few tiny mistakes along the way.

but (b) you probably don't want to try acceleration tests near to alligator-infested swamps in it…

Richard Hammond

Man from Birmingham with naturally very white teeth. Lover of muscle cars, Porsche 911s and motorcycles. While presenting *Top Gear*, Richard has survived a number of death-defying stunts, including being struck with lightning and running with bulls. But he's never managed to conquer his fear of weird foreign food…

133

Rocking chair

Comfy chair loved by old people around the world. Tipping gently back and forth in a rocking chair is one of the most relaxing ways to spend an afternoon… unless Jeremy's hooked it up to a noisy V8 engine!

> Normally the accelerator would be on the rocking chair . . .

Rolls-Royce

British maker of the most luxurious cars in the world, now owned by BMW. Ever since it was established way back in 1906, Rolls-Royce has been renowned for building huge, leathery limousines ideal for wafting from your country estate to your urban penthouse in wafty elegance. The modern Rolls-Royce Phantom is one of the biggest, heaviest and most expensive cars made: it measures over six metres long, weighs nearly three tonnes and costs well over £300,000. Even back in the 1950s, a journey on-board a Rolls-Royce was so relaxing and hushed that the company advertised itself with the slogan: 'At 60mph, the loudest noise comes from the electric clock'. Today, the loudest noise in a Rolls-Royce comes from James May in the passenger seat complimenting its ride quality…

Rolls-Royce Corniche Coupé

Big limousine first built in 1971, as owned by James May. When challenged by the *Top Gear* producers to test his car against Jeremy's old 'Grosser' Mercedes, James though it'd be a good chance to demonstrate how much better his purchase was than Clarkson's. But after a day of getting stuck in London and breaking down, he concluded it might not be the perfect classic car after all…

Romania

Eastern European country famous for (a) once having a mad dictator and (b) containing one of the finest roads on the planet, the **Transfagarasan** (*see page 160*)…

Rotary engine

Unusual engine that produces its power by spinning rapidly. The last well-known car to use a rotary engine was the Mazda RX-8, but this sadly died off a couple of years ago as it couldn't pass modern emissions tests. The proper name for a rotary engine is a 'Wankel' engine. Stop laughing…

Royal Mail

British postal service with 160,000 employees and over 30,000 vehicles at its disposal, including planes and helicopters. Can deliver a letter from the Isles of Scilly to Orkney faster than James and Richard can drive the same distance in a Porsche Panamera…

space and so many open roads to play with, you might assume the Russians have built some pretty impressive performance cars over the years. As Jeremy and James discovered, they haven't. This might have had something to do with the fact that, until the early 1990s, Russia was a communist state – and communist states have never been known for producing anything luxurious, fast or beautiful…

Rubens Barrichello

Brazilian racing driver who has competed in more Grands Prix than anyone else in history – over 300 races, in fact. But that's a minor achievement next to Barrichello's real claim to fame: in 2010, he took the Suzuki Liana round the track in 1m44.3 – faster than The Stig.

Russia

Stretching between Europe and Asia, Russia is the largest country in the world. With so much

It looks as if somebody's crashed a motorcycle into the back of a cow.

We've established that communistical cars were not fast, pretty, well-engineered, cheap or reliable.

Ss

Ach, this is so easy!

Saab

Quirky Swedish car maker that sadly died in 2011. Saab began building aeroplanes, but moved to cars in 1949 and rapidly starting inventing crazy, never-seen-before features. Saab was the first manufacturer to introduce safety belts as standard, the first to introduce wipers on its headlights, the first to use turbocharging and the first to put ventilated seats in its cars. Despite once making beautiful, unusual cars, after it was taken over by GM in 1989, Saab fell into decline, making rebadged Vauxhalls that no one actually wanted to buy…

Sabine Schmitz

German racing driver who is (a) amazingly quick around the Nürburgring and (b) a woman. It was Sabine who taught Jeremy to lap the terrifying German race track in under ten minutes in a Jaguar S-Type diesel… and then lapped it forty seconds quicker herself. In a bid to scare Richard Hammond to death, she also took a Ford Transit van around the Nürburgring in just ten minutes…

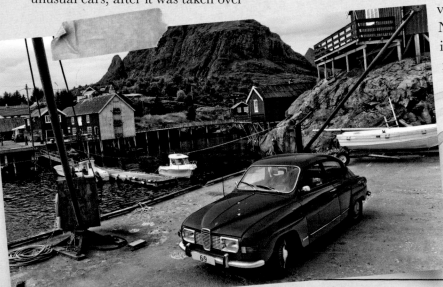

Scissor doors

Doors that hinge upwards from the front of the car, as seen on the Lamborghini Murcielago, the Lamborghini Aventador, and… OK, pretty much every Lamborghini.

Scotland

Cold, hilly country located to the north of England. Scotland is full of majestic mountains that can be conquered in a Land Rover Discovery. At least, they can if your name is Jeremy Clarkson and you don't mind making a lot of people angry.

Seat

Confusingly, both the thing that you park your bum on while driving, and also a Spanish manufacturer of cheap-ish cars. Technically you're supposed to write the Spanish car company as SEAT, but this makes it look as if you're shouting. Seat (the car company, not the bottom-cushion) is owned by VW and their cars are closely related: the Ibiza shares many parts with the Polo, while the Leon is very similar to the Golf…

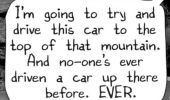

I'm going to try and drive this car to the top of that mountain. And no-one's ever driven a car up there before. EVER.

A B C D E F G H I J K L M N O P Q R **S** T U V W X Y Z

I'm now going to push this little button on the steering wheel here and it's going to set off . . . at [gulp] race speed!

a book while your car drives itself safely down the motorway... but as Jeremy found out when he allowed BMW's driverless 330i to take him for a lap of the *Top Gear* test track, it's not actually a very relaxing experience.

Self-parking car

Clever technology that allows a car to identify a parking space and smoothly reverse into it without the driver lifting a finger. A nice theory, but most of the time it doesn't quite work like that...

Sebastien Vettel

German racing driver and winner of the F1 drivers championship in 2010 and 2011 with Red Bull. Vettel is the fastest driver to come out of Germany since a certain Michael Schumacher, and proved it by blasting the Suzuki Liana around the *Top Gear* test track in a record time of 1m40.0 in 2011.

Self-driving car

A vehicle capable of accelerating, braking, steering and changing gear by itself, without help from the driver. Sounds like a lovely idea, doesn't it? Sitting back, relaxing, maybe reading

I'm not doing anything, I'm not doing anything! It's just the car!

You've hit the Cool Wall!

The power steering pump's really on it's last legs, I've got a terrible wheel wobble . . . but I'm cool!

its triangle of runways was hosting Formula One races. In the last sixty years, the Silverstone track has become ever-longer and trickier: as Richard discovered when he tackled it in a Renault F1 car, it's tough enough just to get round without spinning off into the grass.

Shower

Unusual in-car accessory, as designed by Jeremy Clarkson in his Camaro on *Top Gear*'s Deep South USA Road Trip.

Silverstone

English motor racing circuit and home of the British Grand Prix. Silverstone was built as a military airfield in the 1940s, but by the 1950s

Simon Cowell

Badger-haired X-Factor judge and one of the quickest guests to lap the *Top Gear* circuit in both the Suzuki Liana and Chevrolet Lacetti.

Though skiing is obviously a hugely inferior mode of transportation when compared to the car – after all, it uses gravity rather than good old petrol power – Richard discovered it was a rather faster way of getting down a French mountain than using an Audi RS6.

Ski jumping

One of the silliest sports ever created, in which people wearing lycra and huge skis launch themselves off a giant ramp and hope to land on the snow beneath without breaking into a thousand pieces. *Top Gear* decided this sport would be greatly improved by replacing the skier with a rocket-powered Mini.

Skiing

Method of descending a snowy mountain by attaching razor-edged wooden planks to one's feet.

Concentrate Hammond, concentrate. One patch of ice and I'll be falling for weeks.

Skoda

Czech car maker once famous for building unreliable, leaky cars with all the luxury of a prison cell. But, now owned by VW, Skoda builds brilliantly reliable and good-value cars. All of which is jolly good news, but a bit sensible for the *Stigtionary*. At least it was until Jeremy got his hands on the…

Skoda Yeti

Small SUV that, in Clarkson World, is faster than a Ferrari 308, smooth enough to run a tattoo parlour from its back seat, and strong enough that a helicopter can land on its roof. Helpful consumer advice, Jeremy.

There's a million things that can go wrong with this, and all of them end up with a fireball and me with no head.

Small Japanese Off-Roader Hunting

Since the UK banned fox hunting, what are all those hounds and horses and men in red coats supposed to do with their weekends? To solve this pressing issue, Jeremy invented Small Japanese Off-Roader Hunting, in which a fearsome pack of stallions and dogs pursues a tall man driving a Daihatsu Terios across the countryside.

Snowbine

A brilliant *Top Gear* invention that joins together the best bits of the combine harvester and the snow plough. While most *Top Gear* inventions are rubbish – the Renault Espace convertible, for example – the snowbine is genuinely useful. As the boys proved when they took their homemade creation to Norway, the snowbine will clear a snowy road in record time… and with only minor damage to passing cars.

Ooh, hang on – my flamethrower's jammed.

Smart

Mercedes brand dedicated to making cars so small that they'll fit into motorbike-sized parking spaces. Occasionally Smart attempts to build a slightly bigger car, like the…

Smart ForFour

Dinky four-seater city car that, as James and Richard discovered, is not a very nice place in which to spend twenty-four hours together.

Mate, I'm gonna have to go. I'm sorry. Need a wee.

Smoothie

In the normal world, a drink made by whizzing up fresh fruit in an electric blender. To Jeremy, a drink made by whizzing up beef, Tabasco and a brick in a blender powered by a huge, noisy V8 engine.

It's put hair on my eyeballs!

and can sometimes be so subtle that you wouldn't even notice them. But *Top Gear*'s favourite sort of spoiler, of course, is a massive rear wing…

Space shuttle

It's tough enough to make a rocket that'll blast into space, but to make a space shuttle – a ship that'll go into space AND return safely to Earth – is tougher than teaching algebra to a spaniel. No wonder, then, that when *Top Gear* was tasked with designing a space shuttle around a Reliant Robin, things didn't go exactly to plan.

Speed limit

The maximum speed at which you're allowed to drive in a country. Different nations have different speed limits: in the UK it's 70mph on motorways, while in some states in the USA you can drive at 80mph. In India you're only allowed to do 55mph, but on some German autobahns there's no speed limit at all.

Spoiler

An aerodynamic aid designed to keep a car more stable at speed by smoothing air-flow over its body. Spoilers can be found on the front, back, top or sides of a car,

Spyker

The Dutch are famous for their relaxed, fun-loving attitude to life. So it's no surprise that Spyker – the Netherland's only supercar company – makes some pretty far-out cars. 'I've never seen anything like this before!' exclaimed Jeremy when he gazed on the glitzy interior of the Spyker C8 back in 2004. 'It's stunning! It's like sitting in a fashion accessory!'

> One of the backers behind the Spyker project is the guy that came up with Big Brother.

You can make your own jokes, right?

SSC Ultimate Aero

American hypercar that briefly stole the production car speed record from the Bugatti Veyron when it hit 256mph in Washington state in 2007. It was an amazing achievement from the tiny American company, and one that didn't impress Bugatti. In 2010, it unleashed the 1200bhp Veyron Super Sport to reclaim its record. The Veyron cracked 268mph, but SSC says it has something even faster up its sleeve…

SsangYong

Korean manufacturers used to be a bit of a joke, but then Kia and Hyundai started making Really Quite Good Cars. This was a bit of a disappointment for television shows that like being rude about rubbish cars, but thankfully SsangYong is still making tragic, ugly cars for *Top Gear* to take the mickey out of. One of them is called the Rexton. Another is called the Rodius.

Steam locomotive

Type of train driven by steam pressure. Steam locomotives burn

either coal, oil or wood, the heat from which turns water into steam and turns its engines. In the 1800s, steam engines were the fastest vehicles on the planet, but have since been outclassed by petrol, diesel and electric transport. Even so, as a sooty Jeremy proved on *Top Gear*'s race from London to Edinburgh, a steam train is still faster than a motorbike from 1948.

Stelvio Pass

Italian mountain pass, one of the highest roads in Europe, and one of the best places to drive in the world. At its height, the Stelvio Pass reaches 2757 metres, rising nearly 1800 metres from the valley floor and including a massive forty-eight hairpins! The Stelvio Pass was built in the 1820s, and has been a holy place for car drivers for over a century. When Jeremy, James and Richard set out to find the best driving road in Europe back in 2007, they declared the Stelvio to be the ultimate location. However, after visiting Romania in 2009, they concluded the Transfagarasan might be even better.

Stig, The

Top Gear's tame racing driver and international man of mystery. What does he look like under that helmet? Does he even have a face? Where does he live? How does he always know when to conveniently arrive in a distant country to test out a supercar? No one, not even the world's cleverest boffins, know the answers to these questions. Some say he once wrestled an elephant to the ground using the power of his mind, and that he invented Branston Pickle, and that his watch goes up to fourteen, and that he drinks by sucking the moisture out of ducks. All we know is… they call him The Stig.

Studio, The *Top Gear*

Drafty aircraft hangar in the depth of Surrey where, once a week or so, three grumpy men and a few hundred *Top Gear* fans assemble to make a telly show about cars. Located

next to the *Top Gear* test track in a top secret location just off the A281 near Cranleigh, the *Top Gear* studio is furnished with very expensive works of automotive art including a bashed-up Toyota Hilux on a plinth, and a sofa made from the tatty chairs from a second-hand car. If you thought making television was full of glamour and bright lights, a visit to the dusty *Top Gear* studio will change all that.

Subaru

Japanese manufacturer very keen on both four-wheel drive and turbocharging. This combination means that Subaru is very good at building (a) tough SUVs capable of chugging over muddy fields and (b) loony rally cars capable of sliding around in the snow. *Top Gear* is obviously more interested in (b), which is why our favourite Subaru is the…

Subaru Impreza

Four-wheel drive rally-car-for-the-road that, for the last couple of decades, has been

engaged in a bruising fist-fight with the Mitsubishi Lancer Evo. Last time *Top Gear* lined the two up, the Evo came out on top… but only just.

Subaru Legacy Outback

Large Japanese car that, according to James May, is 'perfect for aristocrats with children called Reginald.'

Sumo wrestling

Japanese sport in which chubby fighters wrestle each other in a ring. As James discovered when he chauffeured a sumo wrestler and his manager across Tokyo, these fighters are not fooled by cheap Japanese cars pretending to be Rolls-Royces…

They've both got four doors, big boots, and they're both as reliable as a Swiss bus driver's Austrian pacemaker. What more could you possibly want?

149

Supercar

Defining a supercar is like defining the word 'beautiful' or 'art': almost impossible to explain, but you'll know it when you see it. People will argue for days over whether cars like, say, the Nissan GT-R or the Audi R8 are TECHNICALLY supercars or sports cars, but the truth is that you can't define a supercar simply by how much power it produces or how fast it goes. The real way to find out is this: if it makes grown men act like small children when it drives past them down the street, it's a supercar. Just like the Ferrari 458…

Supercharging

Like turbocharging, supercharging is a clever way of getting more power from an engine without making it bigger or adding extra cylinders. A supercharger uses the power of the engine to run a turbine, forcing more air into its cylinders to boost power. Superchargers are less popular than turbochargers, but still feature on a handful of production cars, including the Range Rover Sport and the Jaguar XKR.

> The 458 is one of the all-time greats. It really is absolutely, unbelievably, mesmerisingly brilliant.

All this weight – it spoils the acceleration, ruins the fuel consumption, upsets the handling . . . and getting rid of it makes everything better!

Superleggera

Italian phrase for 'super-light' used by Lamborghini on its most extreme, no-luxury supercars – for example the Gallardo Superleggera driven by Jeremy on the Stelvio Pass...

Suspension

The complex system of springs, shock absorbers and bendy metal bits that connects the main body of a car to its wheels. The design of a car's suspension determines whether it will be a big wallowy pudding or so stiff that it'll turn your spine to powder when you go over a speed bump. The effectiveness of a car's suspension is a big factor in how quickly it'll go round a race track: a car with good suspension will allow the driver to thrash it right to the limit, but a car with rubbish suspension will probably chuck him straight into the gravel.

Urrgh . . . Aargh . . . Uh– AAARGH! Uh . . .

Suzuki

Japanese manufacturer that mainly makes (a) Reasonably Priced Cars, (b) tiny cheap 4x4s capable of escaping from the Bolivian jungle and (c) the cheapest car on sale in the UK, the £6,000 Suzuki Alto. Though its road cars tend to be a touch boring, Suzuki occasionally wheels out a daft concept, like the swoopy Kizashi.

Suzuki Liana

Top Gear's former Reasonably Priced Car. Apart from this, there is nothing else interesting to report about the Suzuki Liana. Ooh, apart from this: Liana apparently stands for 'Life In A New Age'. Is that interesting? No, thought not…

Suzuki Vitara

Small Japanese SUV which, as Hammond discovered, is officially the best cheap police car in the world.

Switzerland

Mountainous European country with very strict speed limits and ENORMOUS fines for driving too fast. So if it's such a rubbish place to drive, why is Switzerland in the *Stigtionary*? Well, because it's home to Rinspeed, a daft Swiss company that specialises in creating cars that the rest of the world thought were too stupid to bother building: for example,

It's unmistakably a doormat with some nails stuck in it.

I think we've finally done it. We've found what has got to be the maddest car in the world!

the water-skimming Rinspeed Splash tested by Richard in 2004.

Syria

Sandy country bordering Iraq, and visited by Jeremy, James and Richard on their Middle East special in 2010. When they reached the country, the boys discovered that *Top Gear* is incredibly popular in Syria, which presented a bit of a problem. Why? Because their destination was Israel and – because Israel and Syria don't get on very well – if Israel discovered *Top Gear*

had been in Syria, they wouldn't let them in. So Jeremy decided the only way to get across Syria was to 'sneak' across the desert. This would have been a lot easier if Jeremy hadn't painted his car in multi-coloured stripes…

Find a garage, a workshop . . . modify the cars for desert sneaking.

Tt

in a situation where things have gone just a little bit off-track: for example, where you've run out of fuel or got a flat tyre. 'That's not gone well' should be reserved for the very worst situations: for example where you've accidentally blown up the whole of the United Kingdom or set fire to the Queen…

Teeth whitening

Method of dental bleaching definitely not used by Richard Hammond.

That's not gone well

Jeremy-speak for 'That's gone very badly indeed'. 'That's not gone well' should never be used

Tom Cruise

Super-famous Hollywood megastar, best known for (a) appearing in smash hit movies like *Top Gun* and *Mission:Impossible* and (b) doing a lap in *Top Gear*'s Reasonably Priced Car alongside fellow movie star Cameron Diaz. Cruise set a then-record lap time

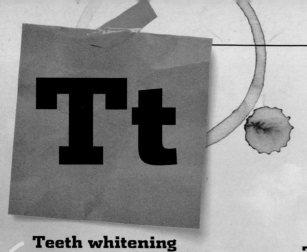

of 1m44.2, though this did involve him taking a corner with the Kia Cee'd on two wheels.

Top Gear Dog

Fluffy Labradoodle who first appeared on *Top Gear* in 2006. After a number of Oscar-winning performances including 'wearing **Doggles**' (*see page 46*) and 'going on a camping holiday', *Top Gear* dog was retired from television but continues to live happily with Richard Hammond and **Oliver** (*see page 114*) somewhere in Wales.

Top Gear Production Office, The

High-tech, cutting-edge production facility where motoring telly magic is made. And definitely not a leaky, rotting green Portakabin on the edge of an industrial estate in Surrey.

Top Gear test track

Secret race track located in a classified location just off the A281 in Surrey. The *Top Gear* test track is 1.75 miles long and was designed by Lotus to test every aspect of a car's handling. The *Top Gear* test track traces a figure of eight, which is just one of the reasons it's never been chosen to host a Formula One race: all the cars would crash into each other as they reached the crossover! Nobody knows the *Top Gear* test track better than The Stig: some say his face is a perfect outline of the circuit...

A B C D E F G H I J K L M N O P Q R S **T** U V W

Torque

Measure of engine power that only James May really understands. Usually calculated on the strange scale of foot-pounds – or 'torques' as Jeremy calls them – torque measures the force at which an engine spins. This is sort of the same as power… but not quite: engines will produce maximum torque at much lower revs than maximum power. In fact, horsepower is actually calculated by multiplying an engine's torque by the speed it's spinning (rpm). Confused yet? Us too. Here's the easiest way to explain it: when you accelerate from a standing start, it's really the torque rather than the power that pushes you back in your seat…

Touring Cars

Type of racing that uses souped-up versions of normal road-going cars. There are literally hundreds of touring car series held around the world, from Argentina to Russia to Germany. But *Top Gear*'s favourite touring car series is the British Touring Car Championship (BTCC), which has seen racing versions of Volvo estates, Vauxhall Vectras and Seat Leons smash each other to pieces around a track in the name of racing. Because that's the most important thing about touring car racing: lots and lots of crashes.

Toybota

Jeremy's name for his amphibious Toyota pick-up truck. Unfortunately

the name was rather
better than the car itself, which turned
upside-down before it could reach the
other side of the lake.

Toyota

Japanese company that fights with
General Motors for the title of Biggest
Car Maker On The Planet. Toyota is
renowned for making very sensible,
very reliable cars that are more boring
than a double-maths lesson. It wasn't

always like this: once upon a time,
Toyota built excellent sports cars like
the Celica and the MR2.

Toyota Corolla

The most popular car in the world,
with nearly forty million cars sold
since it first went on sale in 1966. Also
very boring.

Toyota Hilux

The toughest car on the planet. *Top Gear* has crashed the Hilux into a tree, driven it into the sea, set it on fire, driven it to the edge of a volcano, taken it to the North Pole and even had it demolished with a block of flats, but each time the super-tough pick-up truck has somehow continued working. In honour of its amazing hardiness, a battered Hilux now has pride of place on a permanent plinth in the *Top Gear* studio…

What do you have to do to kill one?

Toyota Prius

Ultra-economical family **hybrid** (*see page 70*) that, as Jeremy proved, actually uses more fuel than a BMW M3 when driven around a race track…

Blip of throttle, lot of smoke . . . Ha haa! It's a MAD car!

Traction control

Clever electronic trickery that stops a car's wheels from spinning unnecessarily. This is a very sensible idea if you are inching up a frozen mountain road and don't want to fall off the side, but not such a good idea if you're trying to to **drift** (*see page 46*) a Mercedes SLS around a circuit. That's why Jeremy turns off traction control before he tests any car on the track.

Train

A connected series of vehicles that run on a track, providing transport for passengers and cargo. Trains can be powered by electricity, diesel or steam, and speed across countries at hundreds of miles an hour or crawl up mountains at a snail's pace. As Jeremy proved in 2011, you can even make a train using a Jaguar XJ-S. It won't be a very comfy ride for the passengers, though…

That's the most amazing road I've EVER seen.

Transfăgărăşan

Impossible-to-pronounce mountain pass that, as *Top Gear* discovered on its Romanian road trip, might just be the best road in the world. Though it was built by a mad dictator, the Transfagarasan does have a few redeeming qualities: perfect tarmac, stunning views, and corners lifted from the greastest race circuits on the planet. The only question is: which car would you most like to drive on the Transfagarasan? Will it be a Ferrari California, an Aston DBS Volante or a Lamborghini Gallardo Spyder?

Triumph Herald

Less-than-brilliant British two-door sports car that, as James May discovered, made no more sense as a wind-powered amphibious vehicle than it did on the road.

Come on, wind!

Turbocharging

A clever method of extracting more power from an engine. Turbochargers use a car's exhaust gases to drive a turbine that forces more air into an engine, increasing power. The biggest problem with turbocharged engines is something called 'turbo lag', which is the time the turbocharger takes to spin up to speed after you've planted your foot on the accelerator pedal. In older engines, this could be a gap of several seconds.

Tyres

One of the most important bits of a fast car. They might all look the same – black and rubbery – but the difference between sticky race tyres and sensible road tyres can make a difference of literally dozens of seconds over a lap.

TVR

British manufacturer that, in the 1990s and early 2000s, built a load of extravagant, noisy and totally unreliable sports cars including the Cerbera, the Tuscan and Sagaris. TVRs weren't suitable for nervous drivers: most of them didn't include airbags or traction control. Sadly TVR hasn't built a new car since 2006…

Uu

Historic People Carrier Race Series suffer from very bad understeer.

Understeer

The opposite of oversteer and much less entertaining. Understeer is a common problem in front-wheel drive cars, and can be seen when a driver tries to accelerate round a tight corner and the front wheels 'wash wide' rather than clinging to the inside of the bend. Most cars in the

USA

Big country on the wrong side of the Atlantic that contains precisely no corners and lots of very long, straight, empty roads. This explains why American cars are very good at going fast in a straight line but have a bit of a problem when it comes to going round corners. The USA is home to three of the biggest car companies in the world – GM, Ford and Chrysler – and was, in the early 20th century, the birthplace of the mass-produced car. Americans have never really understood the rest of the world's obsession with motorsports like rallying and

OK, tame the understeer . . . I've got it! No I haven't! I meant that.

Formula 1, and instead prefer watching hundreds of identical cars going round and round in circles for hours on end. Or **NASCAR** (*see page 108*), as it's better known.

Usain Bolt

Jamaican sprinter who's the fastest man on the planet, and holder of the 100-metre and 200-metre world records. And, as he proved when he got behind the wheel of the Reasonably Priced Car, Bolt is no slouch in a Chevrolet Lacetti either, setting a lap time of just 1m46.5.

Running long distances you get something called lactic acid – you probably wouldn't know.

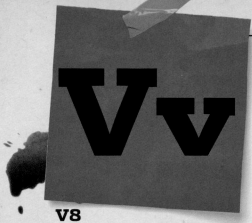

Vv

V8

Type of engine that has been scientifically proven to be Better Than Any Other Sort Of Engine So There, with two banks of four cylinders in a 'V' shape. If you want to picture a V8 engine, tuck your thumbs into the palms of your hands, then interlock your fingers to make a 'V' shape. That's roughly what a V8 engine looks like

(though a bit more metally and noisier). If you don't understand why *Top Gear* is so obsessed with V8 engines, we shall say only this: listen to the Ferrari 458 blasting around a race track and you'll immediately get it!

Vauxhall

British company that's now part of the massive General Motors empire. In the 1990s, Vauxhall had a reputation for building boring, grey cars that were less exciting than watching the Paint Drying World Championships. But nowadays the Luton-based company builds plenty of good fast cars, including the juicy Corsa Nürburgring that James decided was less fun

'Dear James, hope you have fun taking this to the max. P.S. it was developed at your favourite place in the whole wide world.' Oh God.

than a Fiat Panda (he was wrong), and of course the…

Vauxhall VXR8

Brawny saloon with a 400bhp V8 under the bonnet. The VXR8 is actually built in Australia by Holden, which might explain why it's quite so shouty and hairy-chested…

Verbier

Swiss ski resort that, if you're starting in the UK, is quicker to reach by Ferrari 612 than by plane. This scientific fact was proved by Dr Jeremy Clarkson in 2004.

Verdon Gorge

Canyon in south-eastern France that stands over 700 metres tall. Despite the fact that driving from the bottom to the top of the Verdon Gorge involves a long, winding road, Jeremy still thought that he could manage the ascent quicker in a 414bhp Audi RS4 than a climber could scale the Verdon cliff face. He couldn't.

Do you fancy a bet? A fiver? You're on. Best of luck, chaps.

A B C D E F G H I J K L M N O P Q R S T U **V** W X Y Z

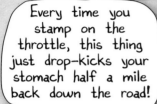

Every time you stamp on the throttle, this thing just drop-kicks your stomach half a mile back down the road!

Veritas RSIII

German sports car with a face like an angry shark. Although it looks like a 1930s race car from the future and has a 480bhp BMW V8 under that long bonnet, you really shouldn't think about buying the Veritas. Firstly, it costs nearly £250,000, and secondly it's a bit rubbish at going round corners…

Video Games

It's a question that anyone who's ever played a driving game has asked themselves: if I'm quick on a computer, will I be quick in real life? As Jeremy discovered when he attempted to beat his virtual lap time in a Honda NSX around **Laguna Seca** (*see page 86*) in real life, the answer is probably 'no'. This might

> The reason crash helmets are small is because people who wear them haven't got a brain.

weird food. Anyone for a snake-meat curry?

Other Important Facts discovered on the *Top Gear* Vietnamese road trip: it is a very good place to buy a cheap, loud suit, but a very difficult place to buy a bike helmet big enough to fit Jeremy's massive bonce…

Vincent Black Shadow

British motorbike first built in 1948. The Black Shadow was capable of 125mph, making it – in its day – the fastest bike in the world. Despite the Vincent's searing 1940s performance, Hammond found it wasn't quick enough to defeat either James in a Jaguar XK120 or Jeremy in a Massive Steam Train in *Top Gear*'s race from London to Edinburgh…

have something to do with the fact that crashing on a computer won't end up with a written-off car and a lengthy stay in hospital…

Vietnam

Large country in South East Asia, famous for (a) a big nasty war in the 1960s and (b) a big *Top Gear* motorbike road trip in 2008. As Richard discovered when the boys pottered nearly 1,000 miles from Ho Chi Minh City to Ha Long Bay on cheap motorbikes, Vietnam is both staggering beautiful and full of really

> The Black Shadow remained the fastest production bike in the world until 1973!

we've forgotten about. Volkswagen means 'People's Car' in German, and was originally founded to provide cheap transport to working Germans. With the Beetle, it did exactly that. Today, Volkswagen and its related brands build over EIGHT MILLION cars every year!

Volkswagen Beetle

Built from 1938 right through to 2003, the original Beetle was the longest-running model ever built, and one of the most popular: over 21,500,000 examples were built in its lifetime. Unlike the 'new' Beetle – which is front-wheel drive and has its engine in the front – the original Beetle was rear-wheel drive and had its engine in the back.

Volkswagen

German manufacturer and one of the biggest companies on the planet. As well as building cars itself, Volkswagen – commonly shortened to 'VW' – also owns Audi, Bentley, Lamborghini, Seat, Skoda, Bugatti and probably a few more

Welcome to the original golf GTi. Now this was cheap, practical, fun and faster than most of the sports cars around at the time.

What were you thinking of, man?

Volkswagen Golf GTi

The original and best hot hatch. The Golf GTi was first built in 1976, sported a 100bhp 1.6-litre engine and would get from 0-60mph in about ten seconds. The modern version has over 200bhp and can do the same sprint in about seven seconds.

Single most tense thing I've ever done!

Volkswagen Polo BlueMotion

Super-economical little diesel city car that can get all the way from Switzerland to Blackpool on one tank of fuel.

Volkswagen Touareg

Huge hippo-like SUV with too many vowels in its name. Jeremy once declared he'd rather eat money than spend it on a Touareg…

We tested it when it first came out . . . and we didn't like a lot of things about it. But this is the brand new Touareg.

Volvo

Swedish manufacturer of massive estate cars so safe that, if you were to crash one into an army tank, the tank would probably come off worse. Fascinating fact: Volvo started out making ball bearings. Actually, that's not a very fascinating fact, is it? Here's a better one: in the 1960s, Volvo built one of the most beautiful sports cars of the day. The P1800 was so cool that it was driven by Roger Moore (who also played James Bond) in TV series 'The Saint'. But Volvo will always be best known for cars like the…

Volvo 940 Turbo Estate

Big boxy estate that, according to Jeremy, is the perfect car for seventeen-year-olds. Many seventeen-year-olds would disagree.

Yes. Yes . . . Aaargh! I can't stop it!

Vuvuzela

Plastic horn popular in South Africa. Made of plastic and makes a dreadful racket. As the *Top Gear* boys discovered, the vuvuzela is surprisingly difficult to play.

VW Scirocco

Pretty VW coupé of the 1970s. Also a pretty VW coupé of the two-thousand-and-noughties.

Ww

An average three-wheeler driver?

Wet

Written on the lap time of a car – or celebrity – if the *Top Gear* test track is rainy or damp at the time. According to information gleaned from the Stig, very wet conditions can add as much as six seconds to a lap around the *TG* track.

Wheels

The circular bits that allow a car to roll along the road. The wheel is believed to have been invented in Europe in the fourth millennium BC, and has amazingly remained the same shape ever since. If your vehicle has two wheels, it's a bicycle or a motorbike. If it has four, it's probably a car. If it has three, it's either a **Reliant Robin** (*see page 129*) or someone has stolen one of the wheels from your car.

Will Young

British singer and the first-ever winner of *Pop Idol* back in 2002. Also Jeremy's favourite pop star.

That looks like six seconds' worth.

Winter Olympics

In the normal world, the Winter
Olympics is an international sporting
event held once every four years and
featuring many brave men and woman
sliding, slipping, falling and jumping
on snow and ice. In *Top Gear* world, the
Winter Olympics is an international
sporting event held, er, once and
featuring a range of good and not-so-
good cars sliding, slipping, falling and
jumping on snow and ice. Oh, and a
rocket-powered Mini…

of the 1980s to Ken Block's smoky new
Fiesta. Over the course of a World
Rally Championship season, drivers
will race on ice, snow, gravel, road and
sand at monumental speeds, often with
cliffs, trees and spectators just inches
from their bumpers. The country most
famous for producing rally champions
is, of course, **Finland** (*see page 56*).

World Rally Championship

The most advanced and fastest rally
series on the planet. Since it started in
1973, the WRC has created some of
the most famous cars in history, from
the beautiful Lancia Stratos to the
fearsome, unlimited 'Group B' racers

F
G
H
I
J
K
L
M
N
O
P
Q
R
S
T
U
V
W
X
Y
Z

Xx Yy

X-Trail

Sensible
Nissan
SUV that
is only in
the *Stigtionary* because we
needed something beginning with 'X'.

Yorkshire

Country in
northern
England
populated by
people wearing
flat caps who
own whippets and drive Reliant
Robins. Thankfully Yorkshire is
also full of friendly

Stig in an X6.
There's the
XC90 too, and
the XKR . . .

Zz

Yorkshiremen who will help to roll your Reliant Robin back onto its wheels when you have gone round a corner a bit too fast – actually, gone round a corner at all – and ended up on your roof.

Zetros

Massive Mercedes truck that'll go anywhere and requires a lorry licence to drive. The Zetros is mainly included in the *Stigtionary* so we had something to put under 'Z'. Ooh, the Renault Zoe. That's a 'Z', too. And what's the Pagani Zonda doing under 'P'?

TopGear
STIGtionary